Church of Christ, Norfolk

The Clergy
of
Litchfield County
|Connecticut|

Arthur Goodenough

HERITAGE BOOKS
2012

HERITAGE BOOKS
AN IMPRINT OF HERITAGE BOOKS, INC.

Books, CDs, and more—Worldwide

For our listing of thousands of titles see our website
at
www.HeritageBooks.com

A Facsimile Reprint
Published 2012 by
HERITAGE BOOKS, INC.
Publishing Division
100 Railroad Ave. #104
Westminster, Maryland 21157

Copyright © 1909 Arthur Goodenough

This volume is one of a series originally published under the auspices of the Litchfield County University Club
1909

— Publisher's Notice —
In reprints such as this, it is often not possible to remove blemishes from the original. We feel the contents of this book warrant its reissue despite these blemishes and hope you will agree and read it with pleasure.

International Standard Book Numbers
Paperbound: 978-0-7884-2700-8
Clothbound: 978-0-7884-9146-7

PAR AVANCE

This volume is one of a series published under the auspices of the Litchfield County University Club, and in accordance with a proposition made to the club by one of its members, Mr. Carl Stoeckel, of Norfolk, Connecticut.

HOWARD WILLISTON CARTER,
Secretary.

CONTENTS

CHAPTER		PAGE
I	FOUNDATIONS	3
II	THE PIONEERS	10
III	MANNERS AND CUSTOMS	18
IV	AN EIGHTEENTH-CENTURY SERMON	29
V	BIOGRAPHIES	39
	Rev. Joseph Bellamy	40
	Rev. Azel Backus, D.D.	42
	Rev. John Trumbull	43
	Father Mills	45
	Rev. Daniel Farrand	48
	Rev. Ammi Ruhamah Robbins	50
	Extract from the Autobiography of a Blind Minister, Timothy Woodbridge	53
	Rev. Peter Starr	55
	Rev. Nathaniel Roberts	56
	Rev. Cotton Mather Smith	58
	Rev. Jeremiah Day, D.D.	61
VI	SECOND PERIOD—TRANSITION	65
VII	PERSONAL SKETCHES	74
	Rev. Stanley Griswold	74
	Rev. Alexander Gillett	77

CONTENTS

CHAPTER		PAGE
	Rev. Asahel Hooker	80
	Rev. Luther Hart	81
	Rev. Samuel R. Andrew	82
	Rev. James Beach	83
	Rev. Chauncey Lee, D.D.	85
	Rev. Frederick Marsh	88
VIII	THIRD PERIOD—MODERNISM	95
IX	MORE PERSONAL SKETCHES	99
	Rev. Joseph Eldridge, D.D.	99
	Rev. Adam Reid, D.D.	101
	Rev. Lavalette Perrin, D.D.	103
	Rev. William Elliott Bassett	105
	Rev. Hiram Eddy, D.D.	107
X	THE EPISCOPAL CHURCH	110
	Bethlehem	115
	Bridgewater	116
	Canaan	117
	East Plymouth	118
	Harwinton	119
	Kent	120
	Lime Rock	121
	Litchfield	121
	Marbledale	130
	New Milford	131
	Northfield	136
	Pine Meadow	137
	Plymouth	138
	Riverton	140

CONTENTS

CHAPTER		PAGE
	Roxbury	141
	Salisbury	142
	Sharon	144
	Thomaston	145
	Torrington	145
	Washington	146
	Watertown	147
	Winsted	148
	Woodbury	149
XI	BAPTISTS	154
XII	THE METHODISTS	160
	Preachers	166
	Stationed Preachers	167
	Presiding Elders	168
XIII	THE CLERGY AS CITIZENS	170
XIV	THE CLERGY IN LITERATURE	177
XV	WIT AND HUMOR	186
XVI	MINISTERS' CHILDREN	195
	APPENDIX	203

LIST OF ILLUSTRATIONS

Church of Christ, Norfolk	*Frontispiece*	
Congregational Church, New Milford	facing page	12
Lyman Beecher	"	18
Congregational Church, Town Hill, New Hartford	"	30
Ammi Ruhamah Robbins	"	50
Horace Bushnell	"	66
Congregational Church, Goshen	"	74
Frederick Marsh	"	88
Joseph Eldridge	"	100
Lavalette Perrin	"	104
Congregational Church, Salisbury	"	116
St. Michael's, Litchfield	"	128
St. Peter's, Plymouth	"	138
Trinity, Torrington	"	146
Episcopal Church, Plymouth	"	152
Methodist Episcopal Church, Winsted	"	160
Congregational Church, East Canaan	"	170
Charles G. Finney	"	180
Austin Isham	"	192

FOREWORD

I AM chiefly to blame for this book, though a committee of good men whose judgment I respected asked me to write it. I ought to have known better, and have often wished that somebody might express his opinion of the enormity of my crime in a way to do justice to my own sense of guilt. The things I have omitted—some of them through ignorance, others for lack of space—trouble me more than what I have done.

The inadequacy is more obvious when I write of ministers in other denominations than my own, and it was greatly to my relief that Dr. Storrs O. Seymour kindly consented to prepare a chapter on the Episcopal clergy. No doubt all readers of the work will share my gratitude to him.

From my own point of view I excuse myself in part for the lack of proportion in treatment by assuming

FOREWORD

that the Congregational ministry was a part of the indigenous element which made Litchfield County to differ from the rest of the world, and so to be worthy of special mention, while those of other name represent the invasion of a cosmic influence that is making us like other people. I have received help and encouragement from so many friends that I dare not undertake to name them here, though they have my sincere gratitude.

ARTHUR GOODENOUGH.

WINCHESTER, CONN., March 5, 1909.

THE CLERGY
OF LITCHFIELD COUNTY

CHAPTER I

FOUNDATIONS

o write of one county among the many counties of this great country may seem a little thing. To give special attention to one class of men in a single county may seem a matter of still less importance. When that county is the county of Litchfield, in Connecticut, and the class of men selected comprises those who for more than a hundred and fifty years have been the pastors of its churches, the question has a new significance.

Men of large information who have lived outside its boundaries have expressed the opinion that in proportion to its years of history and population this county

THE CLERGY OF LITCHFIELD COUNTY

has produced more great men than any other part of the world. Some who live in it are ready to acknowledge the truth of this statement. Among these great men the clergy have always been leaders, and may safely be regarded as an important factor in the production or development of greatness in others.

The causative elements in the distinction of Litchfield County may be regarded as threefold—its physical geography, its race stock, and its time and place in the history of New England.

It is the "mountain county" of Connecticut. The scenery furnished by its hills and valleys, its lakes and streams, is not easily surpassed. Its air is health-giving, and the physical energy called out by struggling with its difficulties for the means of living has been naturally correlated with the development of a corresponding mental and moral force in its inhabitants.

It is said that three kingdoms were sifted to furnish their choicest and best for the beginnings of New England. There was still another sifting before the youngest and most vigorous descendants of the settlers in Connecticut and New Haven colonies took possession of Litchfield County.

It was comparatively infertile and inaccessible and was the last part of the State to be occupied.

Those who came brought with them the Puritan traditions and customs, modified by some generations of

FOUNDATIONS

experience. The clergy had an authority and leadership accepted without question in secular as well as religious affairs. The Congregational ministers and churches were as essential a part of the beginnings of New England as were the towns and the town meetings. In New Haven Colony, church membership was essential to a vote or voice in town affairs, and the town governments were practically organized by the churches under direction of the ministers. The southern part of Litchfield County was settled earliest, and its people were from the New Haven Colony. Woodbury, the oldest of the Litchfield towns, was settled by a church already organized in Stratford, which brought its pastor along.

Congregational principles involve democracy, and lead to the recognition of equal rights for all men alike in religious, political, industrial, and social relations. This fact was not seen nor accepted by the Puritans generally, and they were for the most part thorough aristocrats in belief and practice. They belonged to the English middle class, and there were many among them descended from royalty or nobility.

In the mother-country pastors and people alike had been members of the English Church, and they brought with them their parish customs and ideals. Their ministers were scholars trained at the English universities and belonging to the best English families. The New England people were accustomed to look up to their

THE CLERGY OF LITCHFIELD COUNTY

ministers socially as men of hereditary rank, and of a scholarship beyond the common understanding, as well as dignified by a sacred calling and a position of recognized official authority. The pastors of the churches were practically town officials. They were supported by a town tax, held a life tenure of office, and had a special authority within town or parish boundaries on which others were forbidden to infringe. They superintended the schools, looked after the religious instruction of the pupils, and took charge of neighborhood or family morals in a commanding way now hard to appreciate. It was frequently the case that a town employed its minister before a church was organized, and it continued to pay his salary when he had been ordained as pastor of the church. When once the church had been organized and its pastor ordained, the town could not even by its own vote avoid the continued payment of his salary by a tax levied on all its property-holders. In the case of Stephen Heaton, first pastor in Goshen, the town brought charges against him before the Consociation, and the trial lasted six years before he was dismissed from his office for cause, and the town relieved of his support. It is pleasant incidentally to know that as a lay member of the church and community he was for the rest of his life prosperous and respected.

When we are told that the Puritans came to this

FOUNDATIONS

country to secure the free exercise of their religion, we might naturally infer that the whole population would be alike religious, and free to carry on their religion according to personal taste, but in both respects the inference would be wrong.

The *leaders* were religious—most of them church members—and strenuous in maintaining the Christian life as they understood it, but they were *not* zealous for the liberties of irreligious people, and from the beginning there were many such among them.

They were accompanied by many servants and retainers of a different class from that of which history is accustomed to take account. "Lewd fellows of the baser sort" are occasionally mentioned. They gave tone to the court records and sometimes to the church records of the early days.

Helen Evertson Smith, in "Colonial Days and Ways," tells us that the company which settled Watertown, Massachusetts, brought with them one hundred and eighty servants, whose passage cost the company an average of something over eighty-three dollars each. Of course after the settlements were established the way was open for adventurers of all sorts, who in any way could find the means for crossing the ocean, and they would crowd into every new settlement.

We have no reason to think that in the days when Litchfield County was settled there was ever a time

THE CLERGY OF LITCHFIELD COUNTY

when as large a proportion of the population were church members as in our own days.

There was in every community a large number of "outsiders." Some of them were intelligent, respectable, orderly, and well-to-do people, whose sympathies were with the pastors and the churches. There were many others who were profane and disorderly and not lovers of the dominance maintained by the churches and their ministers.

Church attendance was compulsory on all the people, as school attendance is now on children of school age. Profanity and Sabbath-breaking were severely punished by law. If the squire and the parson were in accord, they looked after the affairs of the community with combined authority, and ruled, if so disposed, with a heavy hand.

If the squire differed with the parson in politics and in social ideals, there was more liberty for the people, but bitter strife between parties, and probably biting and somewhat personal sermons from the pulpit.

It was natural that in the older communities there should be some relaxation of religious interest and of vigor in religious observance after the strenuous life of the first generations had gone by. The Saybrook Platform in 1708 had fixed the creed of the churches for all time, and established permanent courts for church

FOUNDATIONS

government. The position and authority of the pastor in every parish was settled beyond all question. There gradually came about a reversion to the old customs of the English people, and in many communities church membership came to be regarded as a hereditary privilege, or a right to which decent people had a natural claim. Right belief and orderly conduct were often emphasized rather than experiential evidence of conversion or regeneration, and some ministers were inclined to go back to the English Church for ordination and authority.

From 1735 onward there was a somewhat violent awakening from this condition of things under the great revival in which Jonathan Edwards, and afterward younger men like Joseph Bellamy and others, had a prominent part. It was in the time of the great stress and impulse due to this awakening that many towns in Litchfield County were settled and many of its older churches organized. The influence of the time emphasized the religious motive, quickened and directed the religious interests of these pioneers.

CHAPTER II

THE PIONEERS

N 1751, when Litchfield County was organized, there were in its boundaries fifteen churches with pastors. Woodbury was more than eighty years old, New Milford thirty-four, and Litchfield twenty-eight. The other churches and towns were new. The pastors were all young men except in the one church of Woodbury. The churches and towns were newly organized, the inhabitants mainly young people led by young pastors. Pioneering tests old customs and traditional ways of thinking. The French and Indian wars soon followed, and these settlements were on the danger line. Later came the American Revolution, in which many from these towns were actively engaged and several of the ministers served as army chaplains.

It was inevitable that these strenuous days of out-

THE PIONEERS

ward activity and excitement should greatly influence the character of ministers and churches. Personal initiative and responsibility made strong men and compelled original thinking.

In the beginning there was general agreement in theological belief among the accepted religious teachers, and in the first days of religious innovation the credal statements were for a time left for the most part undisputed. Yet the great awakening had brought about a condition of religious ferment in all New England, and the men of Litchfield County took an active part in the readjustments which followed. Whitefield and other traveling evangelists passed through and were followed by departures from old customs and more or less of confusion and excitement. Established methods of parish work were in some cases rudely broken in upon. There were many conversions and additions to the churches from the classes least identified with previous church membership and church control, and religious expression took on new forms.

Under the new impulse young men frequently were impelled to take an active and original part in religious meetings. Even uneducated people felt called upon to give a public expression of their faith and experience.

As nothing corresponding to our prayer-meetings or Sunday-schools was then in existence, it was difficult for a general and strong religious feeling to find vent with-

THE CLERGY OF LITCHFIELD COUNTY

out some outburst that would seem disorderly and awaken alarm or prejudice.

The General Association of Connecticut in 1745 passed the following resolutions: "Whereas there has of late years been many errors in doctrine, and disorders in practice, prevailing in the churches of this land, which seem to have a threatening aspect upon these churches; and whereas Mr. George Whitefield has been the promoter, or at least the faulty occasion of many of these errors and disorders, this Association think it needful for them to declare that if the said Mr. Whitefield should make his progress through this government, it would by no means be advisable for any of our ministers to admit him into their pulpits, or for any of our people to attend upon his preaching and administrations." Notwithstanding this good advice, the Rev. Cotton Mather Smith's pulpit in Sharon was open to Whitefield, and he was probably welcomed in other parishes of the county.

Among the disorders enumerated by the Association with disapproval are: "Intruding into other ministers' parishes, and laymen taking it upon them in an unwarrantable manner publicly to teach and exhort."

These untoward acts of laymen were not only felt to be an intrusion upon the rights of ministers and elders, but as opening the door to false doctrines by permitting unsafe and crude thinkers to teach. Jonathan Edwards,

Congregational Church, New Milford

THE PIONEERS

who was held in great degree responsible for the new order of things, strenuously rebuked the innovations which grew out of the new religious impulse. Even wise men often think to make old bottles hold the new wine. Though no theological change was immediately apparent, the germs of new thinking were being planted and taking root. Joseph Bellamy, pastor at Bethlehem, had taken part in the new movement, but was much disturbed by some of its results. He preached strongly against the incoming disorder, and published books of wide circulation intended to promote an orderly adjustment of the new life to the old forms of belief and practice. He was the great man of his day, and constituted in himself the first theological seminary in our land.

It was largely through Bellamy that Litchfield County became at once the center of the strongest Calvinistic thinking of that age, if not of all the ages. In his plan this thinking was systematically coördinated with evangelistic work and an earnest belief in revivals and revival methods. It was this fact that brought the philosophy of medieval times face to face with the deep practical problems of life, in a way that led to some inward conflicts, such as the world has never seen exceeded. New England theology for the next hundred years was to be a war of giants, and the men of Litchfield County were to be largely the accepted leaders.

THE CLERGY OF LITCHFIELD COUNTY

Many, though not all, of the churches and pastors in this county were in sympathy with the greater strenuousness of religious life which had come in. They insisted on more rigid rules for the acceptance and conduct of church members, and so became involved in church trials and divisions. Frequent dissatisfaction and opposition was aroused in men who wished church privileges on easy terms.

When the pastor and majority of the church held to the more lax and conservative methods of the earlier time, there was denunciation on the part of the new converts, who were no longer willing to sit under the preaching of "unconverted ministers," and sought for relief when possible in some new organization.

The difficulty in organizing a new Congregational Church was especially great. The law of the State already permitted Episcopalians and Baptists to maintain churches of their own, and escape taxation for support of the Standing Order. Those who wished to establish a separate Congregational Church had still to pay their taxes to the older organization until they could be relieved by special act of the Legislature, which could not easily be obtained. A separate church was organized in Canaan, which for a time had more than one hundred members, and which moved as a whole to Stillwater, New York.

Some relief could be found where neighboring

THE PIONEERS

parishes adopted different methods. As, for instance, Torrington followed the Half-way Covenant, while Winchester, a contiguous parish, held to the most rigorous requirements of church membership, and only the children of those in full connection were baptized. In such case trouble was liable to arise because the stricter church would not receive members by letter from the other without a personal examination in regard to the religious experience.

The first pastor in Salisbury, the Rev. Jonathan Lee, was ordained on the basis of the Cambridge Platform, and ministers who took part in the ordination were censured by the association to which they belonged. Though all were supposed to hold by the same orthodox creed, there was a good deal in those days to prevent pastors from settling down into a monotonous condition of quiet and undisputed authority.

Circumstances were favorable to the invasion of religious organizations opposed by the Standing Order. Episcopal and Baptist missionaries entered the field, socially and religiously speaking, from opposite sides. As we before observed, the drift of conservative men in the older communities had been naturally toward the ways of the English churches. Some ministers of standing and influence felt that safety lay in that direction, and that it would be wise to secure ordination from English bishops and return to a full connection with the

THE CLERGY OF LITCHFIELD COUNTY

churches of the mother-country. The churches generally resented this movement with energetic decision as soon as they comprehended the meaning of it, but there continued to be men of prominence who sought relief from the rigid Calvinism of the preaching to which they were compelled to listen, and what seemed to them the inroads of a dangerous fanaticism, by turning back to the English communion.

The Society for the Propagation of the Gospel in Foreign Parts sent its missionaries into New England, and under the auspices of this society parishes were established in Woodbury, New Milford, Litchfield, Plymouth, and other places in Litchfield County. The War of the Revolution was unfavorable to their progress, as they were supposed to stand for England politically as well as religiously, and the patriotism of the vast majority was intense.

On the other hand, the Baptists met the wants of the new converts who wished to introduce and maintain a more emotional type of piety and to protest against the dominance of the governing class in the churches, and what was supposed to be their respectable worldliness.

The Baptist missionaries of the eighteenth century were uneducated men of large enthusiasms, who traveled through the towns gathering congregations in private homes and urging men to a new life by unconventional methods. When in 1798 Stephen Smith Nelson was

THE PIONEERS

ordained as the first pastor of the First Baptist Church in Hartford, we are told in Sprague's "Annals" that he was the only Baptist minister in Connecticut with a collegiate education. Many small Baptist churches were organized in Litchfield County near the close of the eighteenth century or in the beginning of the nineteenth, which in the next generation gave way to the Methodists. We occasionally stumble on the foundations where were formerly their houses of worship. They had a mission of importance in their time, and their influence lives on in other churches, or, it may be, in far-off communities. There are still churches of other names which might well die for the good of the cause which they represent, and which yet have done good work for God in their place and time. A few of these early Baptist churches, like the two in Colebrook, have continued until this day. The theology of the preachers of this denomination was Calvinistic and did not for the most part contradict that preached in the Congregational churches. They were contending rather for the rights of the common people to a larger participation in worship, and to a kind of preaching and teaching more on a level with their tastes and practical needs. The preaching of the old-time Congregationalist demanded study and thinking, and sometimes put a strain on the minds of hearers that could not be patiently borne.

CHAPTER III

MANNERS AND CUSTOMS

WOULD like, so far as my own limited knowledge and descriptive powers permit, to bring before my readers in some detail the customary life and work of a Litchfield County pastor of the eighteenth century. Of course the distinctive work of every minister was preaching. Congregations were accustomed to expect and require two sermons on each Sunday. They were preached forenoon and afternoon, with a recess at the noon hour for visiting and luncheon. As there were no fires in the churches in winter, a recess at that season was also desirable to permit women and children to warm themselves at a neighbor's or in the Sabbath Day House near by.

There were no evening meetings, no prayer-meetings, no Sunday-schools, except that, we are told, Dr. Bellamy

Lyman Beecher

MANNERS AND CUSTOMS

had a Bible class in Bethlehem. There were sermons on Fast and Thanksgiving days, and a lecture on the Friday afternoon before the Communion. Near the beginning of the nineteenth century some ministers took to holding weekly lectures on Friday afternoon, at which neighboring pastors were frequently called to participate. In times of revival more frequent week-day services were held. At the beginning of the nineteenth century we find Dr. Lyman Beecher holding evening meetings each week in different parts of his large parish in Litchfield. About the same time there were neighborhood prayer-meetings started in Winchester, which the Rev. Thomas Robbins, preaching in that parish in 1806, speaks of attending. There may have been other cases of neighborhood preaching or prayer-meetings still earlier, but I have found no evidence of them.

The Rev. Ammi Ruhamah Robbins of Norfolk had a record of about sixty-five hundred sermons in a pastorate of fifty-two years, which implies more than an average of two sermons a week; but as he had been chaplain in the army, and missionary at different times in the new settlements where preaching came in every day, and would have frequent occasions at ordinations and meetings of consociation outside, more than the two sermons a week may not be implied in ordinary service.

There have come down to us reports as to the length of these sermons which I have no doubt are exaggerated.

THE CLERGY OF LITCHFIELD COUNTY

Statements are sometimes made that sermons were two hours long, and the long prayer an hour. I think the people who tell these things did not carry watches, and clocks were not then used in the churches. Undoubtedly much less time in those days was given to other parts of public service than is customary for us, and more time was left for prayers and sermons.

In making our estimate I think it fair to suppose that sermons preached on great occasions and important enough to be published would be longer than the average. Dr. Bellamy preached a sermon before the Consociation of Litchfield County, at Goshen, May 30, 1753, which contains about fourteen thousand words and would very likely require more than an hour and a half in the delivery, but it was an exceptional sermon, showing that he felt it to be a great occasion and had a great respect for his audience. It was probably a similar appreciation of what was required that led the late Dr. Adam Reid of Salisbury to decline an invitation to preach before the Litchfield North Association on the ground that he "felt unable to prepare anything worthy the attention of that august body." Dr. Bellamy's other published sermons do not usually exceed eight thousand or nine thousand words, and would come inside the hour.

Published sermons from popular preachers like Dr. Asahel Hooker, Father Mills of Torringford, or Jere-

MANNERS AND CUSTOMS

miah Day of New Preston, would have been delivered in from thirty to forty-five minutes. I suppose the usual method of preaching was from quite elaborate skeleton outlines, and in extempore expression would take more time for delivery than if fully written out and read, but I do not believe any preacher was accustomed to preach more than an hour at any time before his usual congregation.

As to the matter and form of sermons there is a good deal of sameness among those which have been handed down to us, but of course they were the show sermons, and I take for granted that there were others presenting more variety and originality both in theme and construction.

There was usually an exposition of the text, a logical and in some cases a quite ingenious departure from it to prove one or all of the five points of Calvinism, followed by a review and a personal application to the different classes of hearers. Whatever the beginning, it usually led up to the terrors of hell and closed with a solemn warning.

We have reason to believe that, besides these elaborate discourses, there were actually many of a lighter and more practical character, dealing with the affairs of common life in an effective way. We know that sermons were frequently preached handling public affairs in the style of the Old Testament prophets, giving

THE CLERGY OF LITCHFIELD COUNTY

political advice or rebuking disorder and immorality in the community.

In the War of the Revolution the progress of events gave tone to the praying and preaching in many pulpits. The Rev. Stanley Griswold, a native of Torringford, and pastor in New Milford from 1790 to 1802, not only made a specialty of politics, but led the way in a general secularizing of religion, which brought not only himself but his church into trouble. The writer has a sermon preached by him March 11, 1801, after the election of Thomas Jefferson to the Presidency and Aaron Burr to the Vice-Presidency of the United States. He had voted for the successful candidates and urged others in his party not to take undue advantage of their victory, but to work for peace, and only revenge themselves by kindness for the unmerited abuse which had been heaped upon them in New England. He was dismissed from his pastorate the following year, and soon gave himself wholly to a political life, becoming a United States Senator from Ohio. The trouble with him was not that he meddled with politics, but that he was on the wrong side of politics and opposed to the party to which ministers and leading church members were expected to belong.

From the earliest times ministers considered sermons on all public and social questions to be in the line of their plain duty, and no apologies were needed for instruct-

MANNERS AND CUSTOMS

ing their people in all matters relating to government and good order. Not only was obedience to law and authority inculcated, with due reverence to superiors, but the duties of legislators and officers of the law were proclaimed on the basis of an authority above that of kings and governors. Sermons were preached before the Governor and Legislature laying down the right principles for their guidance.

In Mrs. Stowe's book on "Poganuc People," she mentions the sermons in the parsonage garret, prominent among which was "An Appeal on the Unlawfulness of a Man's Marrying his Wife's Sister." "Then there were Thanksgiving sermons; Fast Day sermons; sermons that discoursed on the battle of Culloden; on the character of Frederick the Great; a sermon on the death of George the Second." This might only indicate that Dr. Lyman Beecher was the leader in a new order of preaching and thinking, which was no doubt true, but we have reason to think that the earlier preachers also dealt with a similar range of subjects in a more restricted way.

Besides preaching, pastoral visiting in case of sickness or special need was expected, but general or systematic visiting of all the parish was not regarded as essential as it came to be in later times in some parishes.

The oversight of the schools and a frequent examination of the pupils on Saturday afternoons in regard to

THE CLERGY OF LITCHFIELD COUNTY

their knowledge of the catechism was recognized as the duty of every pastor. Ministers at their ordination were usually given what was called a settlement, a lump sum paid in advance to enable the pastor to own a house and farm. Hence he was expected to be a farmer, whose land was tilled mainly by servants under his oversight, or that of his wife if she were better fitted for the management of worldly affairs than her husband, as was sometimes the case. The ideal pastor might, like Jonathan Edwards, be so wholly absorbed in heavenly contemplation or theological study that he hardly took note of what was going on in the world about him, and might forget to recognize his own children, not to say his own cows. In that case it was well for "the madam" to be a person of good business capacity who would see that the temporal affairs were wisely looked after, for the most spiritual of men needs to eat sometimes.

It was not, however, unusual for the pastor himself to be a man of common sense who walked on the ground and was able to do business with other men. Slaves or hired servants were usually a part of the minister's family and were used with profit.

Many of the early ministers in Litchfield County were teachers of young men preparing for college or a professional life. Frequently there would be several students boarding in the family. Those were days of large houses and large families.

MANNERS AND CUSTOMS

A sketch of the household of the Rev. Cotton Mather Smith, pastor in Sharon, implies that the mistress of the manse was habitually responsible for more than twenty persons. Similar conditions are suggested in regard to Dr. Bellamy in Bethlehem, Dr. Asahel Hooker of Goshen, Robbins of Norfolk, Farrand of Canaan, Parker of Ellsworth, and others. Not all pastors lived on so large a scale, but being for the most part the man of largest education and influence in the community, he was expected to live as an example to other men of high standing.

Business abilities of a high order were needed, and a good deal besides books and theology came in the way of the eighteenth-century clergy. The first pastor in Roxbury, the Rev. Thomas Canfield, left an estate inventoried at more than three thousand pounds, while the total amount received from his parish as settlement and salary for a pastorate of fifty-one years was only about two thousand pounds. His property was accumulated by good business management of household and farm. He was a successful dealer in real estate, and left several good farms to his children. Small salaries were everywhere a necessity in those days, but there are sometimes other ways of getting on.

I suppose ministers in those days had, as now, their individual methods of studying and preparing sermons, and preached according to their gifts and habits. I find

THE CLERGY OF LITCHFIELD COUNTY

a statement of the method of Jacob Catlin, born in Harwinton, and pastor in New Marlboro, Massachusetts, which I think was regarded by the ministers in this vicinity as ideal. In the noon recess on Sunday he talked with his people and gathered from them themes and texts which they would like to have preached upon. On Monday morning he went into his study, folded paper for two sermons, and wrote a text at the head of each. He then attended to his farm forenoons, and gave his afternoons to visiting the sick, looking after the schools, giving lectures, or doing other outside work, allowing the sermon themes to simmer in his mind. On Friday morning he went into his study and wrote all day on his first sermon, finishing it up at a white heat. On Saturday he did the same thing with the second sermon.

Ministers' libraries were not large in those days. A few books, thoroughly read and re-read, furnished material for a good deal of thinking, even if it were necessarily within a narrow range. Probably as wholesome thinking can be done in the field or on horseback as in the study. The few books needed for a working library would vary, then as now, according to taste. When, after the death of Dr. Bellamy, his library was offered for sale, and some came from a great distance to purchase, they were surprised to find it consist mainly of a collection of infidel works, which he owned for the sake

MANNERS AND CUSTOMS

of controverting them. I once felt a similar surprise when, supplying for a popular minister in this same Litchfield County, I found in his library no theological works but the Bible and Hodge on Romans, by the side of Hoyle's "Games" and some works on hunting and fishing. The aforesaid minister was not very long a Litchfield County pastor, but while reading does help one's thinking in various ways, the amount or kind of reading we do by no means furnishes a measure of our thinking.

Some individual pastors may in this later time have found out the way to indulge in lazy habits. Some were accused of it even in those good old days, but I don't think laziness could have become very general among them. The Rev. Ralph Emerson, D.D., when he became pastor at Norfolk in 1816, did not expect an easy life. He said: "The preacher has before him a life of ceaseless toil, and that of the most exhausting kind. . . . The composition and delivery of sermons is what wears out the life of a minister. The strong tone of feeling requisite for this purpose, joined with the attendant anxiety and effort of mind, shatters the nerves and ruins the health. His labor is not only more exhausting, but is of longer continuance, than the employment of other men. The toils of the body end with the setting sun. It is not so with the mental effort of the preacher. While his parishioners are relaxing from their labors, his mind is at its work; and often, while they are reclining in soft slumbers of midnight, he is at the lamp, with pained head and aching heart, pondering what truths may rouse them from the slumbers of spiritual death. . . . In fact, his spirit knows neither rest nor end in its labors. . . . The Sabbath, ordained by heaven as a day of rest to man and beast, is a day of painful and hazardous exertion to the preacher. It calls him to an effort which has cost many a life." However true this was to Dr. Emerson, I do not believe it has been true of all or most ministers. The Christian faith has enabled many of them to throw off anxiety and rest at the end of a day's work, and the average life of the clergy has been longer than that of their parishioners. They have had plenty of work and great responsibilities, but have not needed pity.

CHAPTER IV

AN EIGHTEENTH-CENTURY SERMON

E could hardly get an adequate conception of the ministers of the first half-century in Litchfield County without a sermon of their times. To print one of their sermons verbatim would be easy, but it has occurred to me that it would be better if a shorter sermon could be made to suggest all the doctrines most emphasized and universally accepted by them. I have ventured to condense and combine two sermons, one by Dr. Bellamy, the other by Asahel Hooker of Goshen, putting the introduction in my own language, but holding to their thought. In this way some violence is done to the unity of the discourse, but I hope that the most usual subject-matter of the preaching is fairly presented in one third the space required for a complete sermon in those days.

THE CLERGY OF LITCHFIELD COUNTY

Dr. Hooker was a disciple of Dr. Bellamy and the leading teacher of theology in this county and perhaps in New England after Dr. Bellamy had ceased from his labors. I think he believed himself to agree thoroughly with what the older man had taught, but he sought newer methods of presentation, and opened the way for the controversy between the New Haven theology and the East Windsor theology, which followed in the next generation between men who had been under his teaching.

Text, Romans ix. 16: "So then it is not of him that willeth, nor of him that runneth, but of God that showeth mercy."

We, looking at things great or small from the standpoint of our own narrow lives, may seem to have some great efficiency or importance in ourselves or in our circumstances. In fact, there is just one great reality, God. All else is but the fringe of his seamless garment. The kingdom and the power and the glory are his alone.

In the unmeasured ages before the worlds were made he alone had being. He was absolutely perfect and sufficient in himself. He had no need of the worlds or of companionship. It seemed good to him to create worlds, and to bring into being spiritual and personal existences with whom he could have fellowship. He did this with perfect knowledge in minutest detail of all that should follow as his worlds rolled onward and the experience of

Congregational Church, Town Hill, New Hartford

AN EIGHTEENTH-CENTURY SERMON

his living beings became history. In perfect righteousness and wisdom he planned and executed. His universe has been, is, and ever shall be the best possible expression to finite intelligence of his infinite perfection. In our time and place we get but a passing glimpse of the dust of his chariot-wheels, yet this is sufficient to bring us face to face with what is to us a great problem, the fact of sin and its consequences.

We are taught by God himself that every sin is detestable, utterly and forever to be condemned, the abominable thing which he hates. Holy angels in heaven sinned and were hurled forever from their seats of power and privilege, cast into chains of darkness and everlasting torment. Man, created holy, was seduced into sin, and rests under a like eternal condemnation, but not without hope. Why sin was permitted in the world we do not know. We may be sure that God could have prevented it, and could have preserved all beings in a state of perfect holiness and happiness with perfect ease if he had seen it best. He chose a world with sin in it and had an absolute unquestionable right to do so. None the less he is in no wise to blame for the sin. It is the free act of his free and responsible creatures, and they alone are rightly condemned and eternally punished for it, punished by helpless and endless torment, beyond all our present conception of misery.

"All the sin and misery that has or ever will take

place in the system through eternal ages, even the whole, lay open full and plain to the divine view, before God created the world; and he had as full, perfect, and lively apprehension of it, before he began to create, as he ever will have to eternal ages." "If God had pleased, he could have hindered the existence of sin, and caused misery to have been forever unknown in his dominions with as much ease as to have suffered things to take their present course." "God . . . did deliberately forbear to interpose effectually to hinder the introduction of sin into his world, when he could have hindered it as easily as not." "Angels and men were under the greatest obligation to love and obey God, and were left to their own free choice; and God was not obliged, in point of justice, to do any more for them than he did. The whole blame lies at the creature's door, and God is righteous in punishing his sin in creatures, according to the declaration of his Word." (B.)

The condemnation of mankind as a whole for the sin of the first man made the foreshadowing of a general redemption through another chosen representative of the race. "As in Adam all die, so in Christ shall all be made alive." All, in the latter case, meaning all who by the election of God and their own acceptance of his grace are joined to Christ as their representative. "Fallen men are capable, *if disposed,* of accepting the great salvation." "The gospel makes a free offer of eternal

AN EIGHTEENTH-CENTURY SERMON

mercy to all who hear it—addressed to beings fully capable, *if well disposed,* of accepting it." Not one man who has ever lived, or ever will live, has been or ever will be *disposed* to accept, except by the special act of God. "Unless he who hath mercy compel them to come in, they will neither be guests at the wedding, nor taste of his supper. Hence the necessity of a merciful divine influence to apply the Christian redemption to the souls of men." "The salvation of men is of God, from the origin to the consummation." "Wicked men are free and accountable in all their evil deeds. . . . That believers are saved by the distinguishing grace of God does in no measure infringe their liberty of moral action. Nor does it lessen in any degree the propriety of their being punished for every deviation from moral rectitude." "Its being of God, that some of mankind were from the beginning predestinated unto the adoption of children by Jesus Christ, and in due time are called by his grace, is no infringement of other men's liberty of doing as they choose; nor hence can it diminish the fitness of their being strictly accountable. Accordingly, they are justly condemned already because they will not come to Christ for life, nor have him to reign over them as their Prince and Saviour."

"The moral liberty of some men cannot be infringed, or at all lessened, by the grace which, without affecting them directly or indirectly, captivates others to the obedience of Christ. Their case is just what it would have been had those who are now saved been left to perish."

"God may be sincerely benevolent in offering that to men which it would not be for his glory and the happiness of his kingdom, and consequently not consistent with infinite rectitude, to impose on them, making them willing to receive it if otherwise unwilling. Punishing them would evidently be doing them personal justice."

"It is in every view consistent and most desirable that God should distinguish such number and persons of mankind by his saving mercy as he pleases rather than that all should be lost, as they would have been otherwise notwithstanding the coming of Christ and the offer of salvation. Hence it is equally so that the whole should have been rendered certain and inevitable by divine decree before the world began. Thus the doctrine of election as maintained by the Holy Scriptures is most benevolent, consistent, and free from reasonable objection." (H.)

REMARKS

I. "How amazing is the patience of God toward a rebellious, guilty world! And how astonishing the divine goodness, which sends rain and fruitful seasons,

AN EIGHTEENTH-CENTURY SERMON

filling their hearts with food and gladness; when hell is their proper place, and the pains of the damned their just desert! God looks down from heaven upon the children of men and beholds the work of his hands combined in rebellion against him, their rightful sovereign; contemning his nature and will, despising his law and authority, and of a temper bad enough to dethrone him and overturn his universal government had they sufficient power on their side." "He has an adequate idea of the infinite vileness, yet he stays his hand and feeds and clothes the wretches that affront him to his face."

"It is in Scripture attributed to the greatness of God's power that he is able to contain himself and to keep back his hand from destroying the God-provoking sinner immediately. And had he not a strength and fortitude of mind infinitely great, it would doubtless be beyond him to bear with mankind a minute longer. Such infinite provocations would be too much for any but an infinite patience."

II. "How dreadful will the day of wrath be and how miserable the state of the obstinate sinner when God's patience shall be at an end and his hand shall take hold on vengeance and render a recompense to the wicked equal to the infinite evil of their sins!" "Now is the time for patience, but when the day of wrath

THE CLERGY OF LITCHFIELD COUNTY

comes God will let all the world see and know how infinitely vile it is for worms to rise in rebellion against the Most High."

APPLICATION

"Every impenitent sinner will at the day of judgment be sentenced to depart to everlasting burnings. Now does it appear reasonable that sin should be so severely punished? In heaven they cry 'Hallelujah! Just and righteous are thy judgments, Lord God Almighty!' But what is the language of your heart? Say, do you approve God's judgment or are you an enemy to it?"

"Is it become natural to you to look upon hell as your proper due, in such sort as that everything in your circumstance, wherein you are better off than the damned, appears a mere pure mercy? Do you appear so in your own eyes as in the sight of God? and go up and down the world wondering at the goodness and patience of God?"

"Is it become natural to you to be afraid of sin? If you know not the great evil of sin, you know nothing yet as you ought to know. You are a stranger to God, ignorant of your own heart and of the deplorable condition you are in, and to this day are unhumbled, impenitent, and unpardoned. Wherefore consider these things, answer these questions, and say what is your state."

AN EIGHTEENTH-CENTURY SERMON

"Oh, how doleful is the state of secure Christless sinners! At enmity against God, rebels against the majesty of heaven, their frame of heart and manner of life a continual despising the Lord! Constant provocation! And yet, alas, they know it not! They little think what is just before them. The day of account drawing nigh; a day of darkness, of gloominess, and of thick darkness, and of great wrath!"

A CONSIDERABLE time spent with the preachers of a century and more ago gives me a deep respect and even reverence for the men. The calm sincerity and courage with which they faced the most awful problems ever dealt with in our human thinking awakens our admiration, but does not compel our imitation. The greatness of their thought of God it would be well for us to study. Their logical and mathematical way of settling theological questions we cannot use, for we have taken to examining the premises before we make our deduction. We believe in a different God and a different man, in a different world. None the less our life has grown out of theirs, and our thinking was prepared for by their thinking. We have reason to be thankful for the honesty with which they sought to justify the ways of God to men. It is not strange that their sermons constantly refer to the unbelievers and opposers of the truth. The wonder is that the preachers themselves

THE CLERGY OF LITCHFIELD COUNTY

were mainly agreed in their doctrinal viewpoint and teaching. Some felt that the problems were too great for them to deal with, and devoted themselves to the practical guidance of their parishes. The leading thinkers threw their whole might into finding a solution of the problems that would satisfy their own thinking and that of their congregations. The theological variety and controversies of the next century grew out of these same problems. They have gone by, and we in our thinking and our preaching are dealing with matters wholly different, but they are problems liable to return and ask for a new solution in a new age. Yet one cannot but think that there was sometimes an unreality and artificiality, growing out of their other-worldly point of view, which, while it weakened the effect of their preaching, gave a needed relief from the strain of their terrible doctrines.

CHAPTER V

BIOGRAPHIES

TAKE it for granted that a book on the clergy must be biographical to a considerable extent. In undertaking a few personal sketches of the eighteenth-century pastors, I find myself confronted by two difficulties. The best-known men have already been well written about in books or pamphlets accessible to those most interested, and my work will be only a repetition. In regard to those less known only meager information, not likely to be of great interest, is within my reach.

The best sketches I have found are those given by the Rev. Abel McEwen, D.D., of New London, in his discourses at Litchfield in 1852, at the centennial of the Litchfield County Consociation, and published in the

THE CLERGY OF LITCHFIELD COUNTY

record of their proceedings. I suppose the publication is now rare and shall take the liberty of quoting from it more extensively on that account. Dr. McEwen was the son of a deacon in Winchester, and gave his sketches largely from his personal recollections of the men. Matter found in many other books is largely quoted from him, often without acknowledgement.

REV. JOSEPH BELLAMY

THE REV. JOSEPH BELLAMY, D.D., was recognized as the great man of his time. He was born in Cheshire, Connecticut, February 20, 1719, and was graduated at Yale College in 1735, when sixteen years of age. He commenced preaching at eighteen years, and took part with Jonathan Edwards in the great revivals of that period, preaching in many places with great fervor and success. He was ordained in Bethlehem in 1738, and had a pastorate there of over fifty years, where he died March 6, 1790.

In the first three years of his pastorate he went about a great deal in revival work, but the revolution in his home parish was one of wonderful power. "He was a man of commanding presence and great power in the pulpit." He established and maintained in his own

BIOGRAPHIES

house the first great theological training-school in the United States, many of the students boarding in his family. It was customary before his time for the young theologue to spend a year or two with some pastor, who directed his studies and used him for service in his parish, but Dr. Bellamy had a large school and regular courses of study. "He received the degree of D.D. from the University of Aberdeen in 1768." "At the age of thirty he published what was regarded as his greatest work, 'True Religion Delineated,' " the purpose of which was to correct errors growing out of the revivals in which he himself had so largely participated.

"The great body of the fathers in this profession who adorned the closing part of the eighteenth century were his pupils. . . . He reigned as a sovereign in his school, still the members of it venerated and loved him. His criticisms were characterized by sarcasm and severity. . . . Dr. Bellamy was in person manly, of tall stature, in the latter part of his life well clothed with flesh. Pious people and those without religion, the learned and the unlearned, the orthodox and the heterodox, united in pronouncing him an eloquent preacher. He had a voice of great power and compass. So well was he acquainted with the things, operations, and business of nature and of common life, on any and every occasion for his imagery he had a storehouse to draw from with

THE CLERGY OF LITCHFIELD COUNTY

which both his cultivated and his rude hearers were well acquainted."

REV. AZEL BACKUS, D.D.

THE REV. AZEL BACKUS, D.D., succeeded Dr. Bellamy as pastor at Bethlehem in 1791 and was a man hardly less renowned. He was born in Norwich, Connecticut, November 5, 1765, and was graduated at Yale in 1787. He maintained at Bethlehem a classical rather than a theological school until he became president of Hamilton College in 1812. He was distinguished as a scholar and as a humorist, but his sermons were not an encouragement to easy thinking and living.

"Soon after his settlement he preached one of his poignant, awful sermons in a neighboring parish. A hearer, alarmed for the young preacher, asked him, 'Mr. Backus, dare you preach such sermons as this at home in Bethlehem?' 'Yes,' he replied, 'I am obliged to preach them in this style; the people have been so long kicked and spurned by Dr. Bellamy that they will not feel gentler preaching at all. This sermon which you have heard is a mere hazel switch; when I am at home I use a sled stake.' His wit nor even his drollery could be kept out of the pulpit. His preaching was of the most popular kind. . . . Almost every occasion reminded him of human depravity and the peril of the

BIOGRAPHIES

soul, of divine grace, its mercy and richness; and lo, his head was waters and his eyes were a fountain of tears. . . . He excelled in repartee and in the delineation of character. When he portrayed the demagogue from the words of Absalom, 'Oh, that I were made judge in the land,' his classmate, Gideon Granger, said to him as he came from the pulpit, 'Backus, had I known what was coming I would have stood up.' . . . The personal appearance of Dr. Backus was impressive and winning: not tall, but of rotund and well-proportioned figure, a massive head, and a face expressive of sensibility, dignity, and intelligence. He received his D.D. from Princeton." (Quotations from Dr. McEwen.)

REV. JOHN TRUMBULL

THE first pastor in Watertown was the Rev. John Trumbull. He was born in Suffield, Connecticut, in 1715, was graduated at Yale in 1735, was ordained pastor at Watertown (then called Westbury) in 1737. "He was a respectable scholar, but acquired and maintained an influence over the people of his charge by his hospitality, generosity, and friendly intercourse with them, perhaps more than by distinguished preaching. For a clergyman of those times he was wealthy. If any parishioner had lost his cow, or any similar calamity,

THE CLERGY OF LITCHFIELD COUNTY

Mr. Trumbull headed a subscription and made the affluent among his people follow his example. A saying was prevalent that if any one of his parishioners turned Episcopalian, Mr. Trumbull bought his farm." (Dr. McEwen.)

He was a large landowner and a good judge of horses. His son was Judge John Trumbull, the author of "McFingal," a poem exceedingly popular in its day. In 1772 Mr. Trumbull was elected a fellow of Yale College, and continued in that trust until his death in 1787. This occurred after a pastorate of fifty years.

It is said of him in Bronson's "History of Waterbury" that he was not a tall but a stout, athletic man. He was sound, shrewd, and humorous. Athletic contests were frequent between the Waterbury and Westbury young men. "In several of these contests Waterbury had proven too much for Westbury. On occasion of the next contest Mr. Trumbull disguised himself and went down to give material aid if necessary. The wrestlers were called in one after another till Westbury was again thrown out, the Waterbury champion having grounded the last of the rival party. When the signs of exultation on one side and chagrin on the other were becoming manifest, a stranger was dragged in from the outer circle of the crowd to contend for the Westbury boys. The parties placed themselves in position and began playing around to find each other's quality. After

BIOGRAPHIES

a little time the stranger, watching his opportunity, caught his antagonist first and threw him upon the outdoor fire which was the center of the evening gathering. Shouts filled the air, and the victor disappeared." When the secret leaked out "it reached the ears of Mr. Leavenworth, pastor at Waterbury, and the next time he met his brother Trumbull he rebuked him for his levity, and censured him particularly for throwing his rival on the fire. Trumbull agreed that he had been guilty of levity, but as for the scorching said he thought it his duty to give Mr. Leavenworth's parishioners a foretaste of what they might expect after sitting under his preaching."

In his will he bequeathed to his widow his negro wench Lemmon; to his son Judge Trumbull, his negro girl Mabel; to his daughter Sarah, wife of Dr. Caleb Perkins of Hartford, his negro girl Peg; and to his daughter Lucy, wife of the Rev. Mr. Langdon of Danbury, a negro girl that was already in her possession.

FATHER MILLS

THERE was one Litchfield County pastor of the old time who was generally conceded to be in a class by himself. Samuel John Mills was pastor of the church

THE CLERGY OF LITCHFIELD COUNTY

in Torringford from 1769 to 1833, sixty-four years, though with a colleague for the last eleven years. He is remembered for his peculiarities, especially for his humor, and in these later times known as the father of the Samuel John Mills to whom the American Board of Commissioners for Foreign Missions owes its organization. There is plenty of evidence that there was a solid foundation of character and worth beneath the peculiarities of Father Mills. He was a wise and successful pastor, popular with his own congregation and liked by his brother ministers. I wish he could have left at least a volume of published sermons. I have no doubt both thought and language would have amply repaid the study of later times. His usual preaching was extempore, and we have but two printed sermons in a book of selections (dating, I think, from 1797, but the title-page is lacking in the book I have). These sermons are a study of the sentiments of Jesus Christ, planned more nearly in accordance with the present historic method than any other writing of his time with which I am acquainted. The style is remarkably lucid, and the amount of thought packed into two sermons is very unusual in any age. Of course the five points of Calvinism are all there—they had to be—but they do not occupy the foreground in the way usual at that time, and are presented in the most practical and least offensive way imaginable.

BIOGRAPHIES

I have been told, by a man who spent his boyhood under the pastorate of Father Mills, that it was his custom, when in the middle of the sermon he lost his grip on his congregation or they grew sleepy, to stop abruptly and introduce a story or some irrelevant remarks until all were thoroughly awake, then to resume the thread of his discourse and go on as if there had been no interruption. Many of his stories are current. I do not need to repeat them. Other ministers of his time found a place for humor in their social life, and sometimes apologized for it as if it were a sin. So far as I have been able to learn, Father Mills was the only man who dared to use it in his preaching, as an intended relief to his congregation. His personal human influence laid a deep hold for good upon many lives.

Mrs. Stowe, in her sketch of Father Morris, has described him, and many anecdotes have found their way into print. I recall one that I have not seen in any publication.

Near the close of a hard winter he was returning from an exchange on Monday morning, when the road was walled on each side by the depths of snow and new drifts, making it very difficult for teams to pass each other. If any teams turned out of the beaten track, a good deal of floundering and perhaps shoveling might be required. He saw men with a span of horses advancing to meet him, when, rising to his full height, he

THE CLERGY OF LITCHFIELD COUNTY

shouted, with his magnificent voice, "Turn out. Get out of my road, or I will serve you as I did the man in the last town." They proceeded promptly to get out of his way. When, after thanking them courteously, he passed by, one of them asked what he had done to that other man. "Oh," said he, "he was contrary and would n't turn out for me, so I turned out for him."

REV. DANIEL FARRAND

ACCORDING to his biographer in the *Connecticut Evangelical Magazine* for August, 1803: "Mr. Farrand was born of reputable and hopefully pious parents, January, 1720, in Milford, Connecticut." His parents moved to New Milford. "He there continued in the business of agriculture during his youthful days. . . . He was uncommonly attached to books, and discovered a great thirst for knowledge." He received the degree of M.A. from Princeton in 1750, and was ordained in South Canaan in 1752, where he continued in his pastorate more than fifty years. He had a family of four sons and five daughters, and, his salary being small in proportion to his need, he was for a long course of years in the habit of preparing young men and boys for college. It is said in Sprague's "Annals" that "as a scholar

BIOGRAPHIES

in the dead languages Mr. Farrand in his day had few equals," and that "he frequently read his chapter before family prayers from the Greek Testament, without it being observed that his eye was not upon an English one"; which might imply that he approved thoroughly of the Authorized Version. "His manners were simple and plain almost to bluntness; and yet such was the dignity of his appearance as to inspire a degree of awe which precluded any attempt at undue familiarity." He was regarded as a sound theologian and a preacher of high rank, but had a holy tone in his delivery that detracted from the effect of his preaching. He was one of the wittiest men of his day, and his humor was unpremeditated and uncontrollable. Dr. McEwen relates that at a public dinner a brother minister asked Mr. Farrand "whether Mr. Sherman (then pastor at Goshen) would be able, by a book which he had recently published, to reconcile the Calvinists and Arminians? The reply was: 'A wolf once saw two rams, retreating from him in opposite directions, and he exclaimed: "Both of you I can catch; one of you I will have; if you will both turn and come to me, I will spare the life of him who first gets to me." They turned, they rushed, and between the heads of the two butting rams the wolf was mashed.'" (Mr. Sherman was soon in difficulty in his parish, and was paid fifty pounds by the town for his resignation. He was a brother of the Hon.

THE CLERGY OF LITCHFIELD COUNTY

Roger Sherman and a man of popular gifts, but Goshen would not stand the slightest tendency to heterodoxy.) It is said that Ethan Allen published an infidel book entitled "The Oracle of Reason," and gave Mr. Farrand a copy to read. When afterward he asked his opinion, Mr. Farrand said that the paper of the book was of rather poor quality, otherwise he would have thought it a pity that so much of it had been unnecessarily spoiled. He was much valued as a peacemaker and an adviser among the neighboring churches.

REV. AMMI RUHAMAH ROBBINS

THE REV. AMMI RUHAMAH ROBBINS was the son of the Rev. Philemon Robbins, pastor at Branford, Connecticut, who successfully maintained his right to be liberal in an intolerant age. He was born in Branford in 1740, was graduated at Yale in 1760, began service in Norfolk in January, 1761, after studying theology with Dr. Bellamy, and was ordained the first pastor at Norfolk, October 28, 1761, which office he held for fifty-two years, until his death, October 31, 1813. May 16, 1762, he married Miss Elizabeth LeBaron, daughter of Dr. LeBaron of Plymouth, Massachusetts, and granddaughter of Governor Bradford, a lady of splendid gifts, who became the mother of thirteen children.

Ammi Ruhamah Robbins

BIOGRAPHIES

A young man of twenty-one years, he began his service with the church when it had but twenty-three members. When he preached his half-century sermon, the whole number of members received had been five hundred and forty-nine. He kept a diary and careful records of his work, and had preached in the fifty years at home and abroad more than sixty-five hundred sermons—an average of one hundred and thirty a year. In his earlier ministry he made five tours of home missionary work in the new settlements of from two to four months each. In these tours he preached one hundred and forty-five sermons and organized three churches. This was the way for pastors in Litchfield County to take their vacation a hundred years ago, before modern methods were discovered.

Mr. Robbins was chaplain in the Revolutionary army in 1776, but after a few months his health was so impaired that he was compelled to return home. Besides these periods of absence, in 1783 and in 1810 he was laid aside from public service for about five months in each year.

He was a talented scholar and prepared a large number of young men for college. Dr. Abel McEwen, born in Winchester, and for more than fifty years pastor in New London, Connecticut, was one of his pupils. James Watson, a native of Goshen and afterward United States Senator from New York, was another.

THE CLERGY OF LITCHFIELD COUNTY

Dr. McEwen says of his former teacher: "It would be difficult to select a minister in Connecticut who has been more popular with the people in his charge, or who exercised over them a more complete and useful control. Bland and courteous in his manners, with a comely figure, a winning face, and constitutional agility, he ruled the old men, being at once their counselor and their boon companion. The young men were his children: the great majority of them were under his ministry born into the kingdom of God. . . . His sermons generally were not elaborated. His preaching was an easy flow of sound doctrine, natural method, warm affection, and simple but playful elucidation. In his sermons and prayers, especially in the reading of psalms, his voice was a charm. The common and the uncommon people said he was by nature a pulpit orator. He might be criticized; he was inevitably admired."

In his later years he was a member of the Corporation of Williams College, and it was through his influence that the young men from towns in his vicinity, who under the leadership of Samuel J. Mills, Jr., started the missionary impulse that led to the organization of modern missions in this country, were at Williams instead of at Yale. Three of his own sons had a college course, two of whom were ministers; the other, James Watson, preached for a time, but lacked health to continue. He tells us that he had preached from passages

BIOGRAPHIES

in all the books of the Bible except the Epistle to Philemon and the Second Epistle of John, showing that he sought a wide range and variety of themes. His orthodoxy was not questioned. He seems to have been faithful to the doctrines emphasized by Bellamy and other theorists of his day, but had a taste for the more cheering suggestions of the New Testament, to which many were afraid to call attention. It was said that he had preached in every town in the State of Connecticut but three, and in a large number of settlements in northern New York and Vermont.

EXTRACT FROM THE AUTOBIOGRAPHY OF A BLIND MINISTER, TIMOTHY WOODBRIDGE

In my fourteenth year I was placed in the classical school of the Rev. Mr. Robbins, pastor of the church and congregation in Norfolk, Connecticut. My new teacher was a hale, fine, spirited old man; was full of vivacity and the pliancy and facility of manner which we often observe in Frenchmen. He had been the pastor of his church from its organization. His congregation had been so intensely engrossed for many years in felling the forests and exterminating the wild beasts that they had found but little time for intellectual culture; and it is probable that their pastor was tolerably satisfied with the demands of the community in the matter of intellectual improvement.

He was a man of genius, and had the natural qualities of an orator. My teacher was greatly respected by his congregation, and was in that region a sort of oracle. He had a loud voice, great fluency, and preached almost extemporaneously. He carried with him into the pulpit a brief manuscript outline of his sermon; and if the next idea in the method of his discourse did not occur to him in the proper order, he seized upon some collateral thought or illustration, and glowed upon it to the surprise and delight of his audience. But, whether erudite or not, he kept up his familiarity with Greek and Latin, and was a good classical scholar. His school had a great reputation as a theater for training boys for college. I was the hundred and thirteenth boy whom he had fitted and entered at some collegiate institution.

When I joined his school, I had a great desire to go to Yale, because Dr. Dwight, my cousin, was president. But Mr. Robbins, though educated at Yale, was one of the trustees of Williams, and was enthusiastic in his preference for this latter institution. He employed all his persuasions to induce me to go to Williams. This influence, joined to the fact that Williams was near my home, determined me to fix on the Berkshire college.

Mr. Robbins was an animated and pleasing teacher. Immediately after morning prayers, he went up into our

BIOGRAPHIES

school-room with his pipe, and spent an hour with us in hearing our recitations of the evening lessons, and in imparting to us his earnest instructions. He entered into the business *con amore*. When he left us in the morning, we were in a fine glow for study; and at eleven o'clock he returned to examine the results of our forenoon's work, and was faithful, cheerful, and amiable. He was, "take him for all in all," a delightful man. His piety was free, joyous, practical, and generous. He cultivated in me an earnest desire for literary excellence.

He had no touch of the Puritan habit of never praising a boy when he did well, but commended me warmly, and I was grateful for it. It fell upon my heart like the dew of Hermon, and I never abused his kindness, but studied the harder for it.

REV. PETER STARR

THE REV. PETER STARR was born in Danbury, Connecticut, September, 1744, and was graduated at Yale in 1764. He studied theology with the Rev. Mr. Brinsmade in Washington and with Dr. Bellamy in Bethlehem, and was ordained pastor in Warren, March 18, 1772, where he died July 17, 1829, after a pastorate of more than fifty-seven years. His first wife was Sarah

THE CLERGY OF LITCHFIELD COUNTY

Robbins, sister of the pastor in Norfolk. He was a member of the Corporation of Yale College from 1813 to September 8, 1818. Dr. McEwen says of him: "He was of moderate size and active habits; well educated, studious, and intelligent, distinguished for judgment and discretion. In theology he harmonized with his brethren in the country who were contemporary with him. His sermons were short, methodical, lucid, and instructive. A very intelligent man bred under his ministry testifies that he never knew him to deliver a discourse extempore, even in a school-house or private dwelling. More of confidence, respect, and affection than Mr. Starr enjoyed, no pastor has occasion to require from the people of his charge. He was cheerful and diffused cheerfulness around him. . . . Two of his sons were educated at Williams College and went into the profession of the law."

REV. NATHANIEL ROBERTS

THE REV. NATHANIEL ROBERTS was born in Simsbury in 1704, and graduated at Yale in 1732. His wife was a daughter of the Rev. Jonathan Marsh of Windsor, and a sister of the Rev. John Marsh of New Hartford. He was ordained the first pastor in Torrington, October 21, 1741, and continued until his death in 1776.

BIOGRAPHIES

He was an easy man in his theology and church discipline, and followed the Half-way Covenant in church administration. The first pastor in Winchester refused to receive members on Mr. Roberts's letter of recommendation without further examination. He was a somewhat eccentric man, characterized by humor peculiar to himself. He was a successful pastor and built up a strong church by his practical wisdom and uprightness. Not given to much theology, as compared with other pastors of his time, he is said to have believed very strongly in the devil, and to have directed his life and preaching quite earnestly to escaping from the evil one and combating his work. It is said that his emphasis on the devil was the occasion of some amusement among the young people, and that one young man in particular took to counting the number of times the devil was mentioned in a sermon and reporting it. This having come to the hearing of Mr. Roberts, he took particular pains to guard himself against his peculiarity. After finishing his second sermon he turned to the young man and said, "I hope no dissatisfaction will be felt with what I have said, for I have mentioned your master's name but three times to-day."

The story is told in Orcutt's "History of Torrington" that one spring Mr. Roberts had tapped his maple-trees, but for several days the sap had not run. On Sunday the favorable weather came on, and the sap filled his troughs to overflowing. "On Monday morning Mr. Roberts was seen going from tree to tree, turning the sap out on the ground with great vigor and decision, and when a neighbor inquired, 'Parson Roberts, what are you doing? Why do you throw away your sap so?' 'Ah! I 'll have nothing to do with the works of the devil,' said he; 'sap, sap, all day Sunday! I 'll have nothing to do with the works of the devil.' "

"There was a very dry season during Mr. Roberts's pastorate, a day of fasting was appointed, and the people were to assemble at the church to pray for rain. At the appointed time the pastor took his overcoat on his arm and started for the church. Some one asked him why he took his coat. 'I tell you I shall fetch her. I tell you I shall fetch her.' And it is said that it did rain before he went home. Like the other ministers of his day, he was intensely patriotic at the beginning of the Revolutionary War, and is reported to have prayed at his public service, 'Great God, we pray thee to remove that Lord North from office, by death or otherwise.' "

REV. COTTON MATHER SMITH

THE REV. COTTON MATHER SMITH was born in Suffield, October 16, 1731, and graduated at Yale College

BIOGRAPHIES

in 1751. He was a year with Jonathan Edwards, sharing his work among the Indians. In 1754 he began his service with the church at Sharon, and about a year later was ordained pastor, holding the position until his death in 1806.

Dr. McEwen says of Mr. Smith: "He was distinguished for amiable temper, bodily activity, graceful manners, industry, and elegant literature. . . . Bland and courteous in manner, sound in religious inculcations, uncompromising in moral habits and requirements, much in his study, and often in the families of his people, he harmonized their faith and social habits, and gained such hold of their hearts that they retained his ministry and gave deference to his counsels to the close of his life. Somewhat acquainted with medicine, but more because he had the heart of the Good Samaritan, he was sure to be with his parishioners when sick, and never by the sick was the presence of a minister more cordially welcomed. . . . A very distressing prevalence of smallpox at one season put all his benevolence, contrivance, activity, and fortitude in requisition. It was winter; houses for the sick could not be obtained; seven hundred persons were subject to the disease within two months. For nineteen successive days and nights he took not off his clothes for rest. Here was something in addition to good preaching to make a minister popular among his own parishioners. . . . Into the memorable campaign

THE CLERGY OF LITCHFIELD COUNTY

of 1775 he entered as chaplain to a regiment in the Northern army. His influence in producing order and good morals in the camp, in consoling the sick, and inspiriting the army with firmness and intrepidity, attracted the attention of General Schuyler, the Commander-in-Chief, and secured from this worthy officer a respectful friendship for Mr. Smith the residue of his life. . . . A polish of style and a sweetness of affection gave interest to his preaching, while fidelity to the conscience of his hearers gave it power."

In his half-century sermon he stated that he had preached more than four thousand public discourses, besides more than fifteen hundred at funerals and other special occasions. Dr. Thomas Robbins says of him: "Mr. Smith was a man of middle size, rather tall than otherwise, and united great benignity and intelligence in the expression of his countenance. His manners were remarkably polished, so that he might have appeared to advantage even at a court: they were a delightful compound of simplicity, gracefulness, and dignity. . . . In his intercourse with his people and with society at large, he was distinguished for his prudence. He never performed an act or uttered a word that was fitted needlessly to wound others, or to impair the dignity or lessen the influence of his own character. . . . He had a good deal of unction in the pulpit, but his manner was simple, natural, and graceful. His views of divine truth were

BIOGRAPHIES

substantially those held by Dr. Bellamy, but his gentle and urbane manner prevented him from ever giving needless offense."

REV. JEREMIAH DAY, D.D.

THE REV. JEREMIAH DAY was born in Colchester, Connecticut, January 25, 1737. He was brought up on a farm, walked three miles to school, developed a great love for books, and was graduated from Yale College in 1756. After some time spent in teaching, he studied theology with Dr. Bellamy, but, having come to doubt his fitness for the ministry, he went back to teaching. In 1763 he became a farmer in the town of Sharon, and married Miss Sarah Mills of Kent, a sister of the Rev. Samuel J. Mills of Torringford. He was made a selectman in Sharon, and represented the town in the Legislature.

After the death of his wife in 1767, he again took up the study of theology with the Rev. Cotton Mather Smith of Sharon. He began to preach at New Preston in 1769, and continued in that pastorate until his death, September 12, 1806. October 7, 1772, he married Abigail, widow of the Rev. Sylvanus Osborn of Warren, by whom he had five children—a daughter, who died in infancy, and four sons, three of whom were graduates of Yale, and one of them its honored president. He purchased a farm in New Preston, which he worked largely with his own hands, but also took his salary, part in work, and another part in produce. His salary was to be seventy pounds a year, but, at the beginning of the Revolutionary War, he gave up five pounds of it, and also himself paid the tax of honest dissenters, so far as it was levied for his salary.

His letter resigning this portion of his salary is worth quoting. He says: "Considering the greatness of the necessary expenses of the country at the present day, and the difficulty of the times, and being willing to contribute my proportion toward the public expenses, to encourage the glorious cause in which we are engaged, I am induced to give five pounds lawful money the present year to this society, to be deducted out of my salary for the year 1776, which is more than two shillings on the pound of all my rateable estate. And I furthermore make declaration and promise that all those who are bound by law to pay rate to me, but profess to be of any other religious denomination from us, if they will produce good and credible certificate that they have paid for the support of the Gospel to the amount of their rates to me, for preaching which they have enjoyed within the compass of the year, i.e., from February 1, 1776, to February 1, 1777, shall in consequence of application made to me for the above-mentioned year receive a full

BIOGRAPHIES

discharge of their ministerial taxes. That they should be required to pay something for the support of the Gospel is reasonable, inasmuch as a preached Gospel is a benefit to civil society, as well as to the souls of men." This rebate he continued for the remaining thirty years of his life. He was a man of solid goodness and sound sense, whose influence reached far. I will quote regarding him from the *Connecticut Evangelical Magazine* for December, 1806:

"In private life, in the domestic relations, Mr. Day afforded as perfect an example as nature has produced since families were formed. To his wife he was all that her fondest wishes could claim or ask; to his children he was the best of fathers."

"In all his intercourse with his people he was grave, serious, and instructive. Wise as a serpent and harmless as a dove, he was one of the most illustrious examples of ministerial prudence. As a divine he had a sound understanding, capable of deep research. . . . With a clear and luminous method, he loved chiefly to dwell on the great doctrines of divine grace and the distinguishing truths of the Gospel. To his brethren in the ministry he was a tried friend and an able counselor. His advice was much sought and improved. Indeed, in this important branch of ministerial duty he may not have left a parallel. Always upright in his views, remarkable for punctuality in attendance on all appointments, and able

THE CLERGY OF LITCHFIELD COUNTY

at once to seize the right point in every question, able to disentangle the most embarrassed subject, clear and conclusive in his reasonings, fellow-members in council always felt themselves honored when they found his opinion coincide with theirs."

He lived to see his youngest son licensed to preach the Gospel and was ready, like the aged Simeon, to depart in peace, feeling that this life had reached its culmination of blessedness. "He frequently remarked that death had no terrors for him and that, if it was the will of God, he did not wish to live beyond his usefulness." His desire was granted, and he passed away in his seventieth year, able to participate in affairs to the last.

CHAPTER VI

SECOND PERIOD—TRANSITION

HERE was little manifest change in the position and work of the clergy of Litchfield County until about 1800, and until that time there was a general agreement in theological belief, a large proportion of the pastors having been students with Dr. Bellamy, or readily conforming to the accepted standard. For the next sixty years many influences combined to work great and continuous changes. First of all was the readjustment of the Calvinistic theology. Calvinism had long been an accepted theory, but it had probably never been used as the staple in preaching as constantly and thoroughly as in the eighteenth-century preaching of this county. It naturally aroused much opposition and unbelief among men outside the church, but in the Congregational churches it had its own way. Con-

THE CLERGY OF LITCHFIELD COUNTY

troversy with the Episcopal Church was not mainly on doctrinal lines, and the early Baptists were in their way as thoroughly Calvinistic as the Congregationalists. The Methodists were now coming in and were aggressively Arminian. The Wesleyan theology was preached with the exaggerated zeal of men not theologically educated and intensely in earnest. New adjustments were sought for by the new thinkers in the Congregationalist ministry, and there were among them many able and energetic men.

The Rev. Asahel Hooker of Goshen took up the work of training theological students, which had been laid down by Dr. Bellamy, and Dr. Backus of Somers. He was supposed to be thoroughly loyal to the older theology, but was ready to enforce it by new statements. Dr. Jonathan Edwards of Colebrook, Dr. Ebenezer Porter of Washington, and Dr. Lyman Beecher of Litchfield, were ready, with Dr. Timothy Dwight of New Haven, to make the essentials clearer by new statements; and their new statements or improvements were regarded with suspicion by many of their brethren. Dr. Beecher had so much confidence in the power of logic to settle everything that he was very tolerant of efforts to reconsider all questions.

Exciting controversies grew and continued, preparing the way for a sharp division which took place over the New Haven theology, as it was promulgated by Dr.

Horace Bushnell

SECOND PERIOD—TRANSITION

Nathaniel W. Taylor. It is difficult in these days to appreciate the differences which were held to be of such tremendous importance for a generation. The center of Dr. Taylor's improvement seems to have been in emphasizing the distinction between *certainty* and *necessity*. It was certain that some people would be damned, but they did n't have to be damned. There was always with them a power of contrary choice, which they were capable of exercising, and they failed, not because of having made a single wrong choice, but because of a permanent wilful refusal of the right. The leader of opposition to this "dangerous" man was the Rev. Bennett Tyler, D.D., who became the founder of the East Windsor theology. Both men were from Litchfield County. Dr. Taylor was from New Milford, the grandson of the pastor there. Dr. Tyler was born in Woodbury and was pastor for a time of the church in South Britain, then, but not now, in Litchfield County. This controversy of old and new school, attended by the Methodist aggression all along the line, reached every parish and made life more exciting to all ministers, but it only prepared the way for a still deeper revolution in theological thinking, led by Dr. Horace Bushnell in the next generation.

Besides the theological movements there was political upheaval which separated church and state and deprived the minister of his secular authority. After 1818 no

THE CLERGY OF LITCHFIELD COUNTY

man could be taxed for the support of a church or pastor without his consent. In some towns or parishes the system of taxation continued by general consent for a time, but democracy in church affairs had made an advance, and, while the pastor might still exercise a commanding influence by virtue of his character, he was no longer an autocrat by virtue of his office.

The world outside had grown larger, and means of communication were continually increasing. Railroads were built, and manufacturing towns grew up in connection with the new means of transportation. There was an influx of a new and heterogeneous population, with a demand for new churches and with new demands on the ministers.

About 1800, prayer-meetings began to be organized among the people, and a new activity was aroused in the lay element, which formerly had for the most part been silent. In a few years church prayer-meetings on Friday afternoons became customary. Dr. Ebenezer Porter of Washington, and afterward Dr. Lyman Beecher of Litchfield, preached on temperance. Temperance societies were organized in which ministers were leaders, and ministers' meetings adopted habits of abstinence. Societies for moral reform were started. The great missionary movement began with young men from this county as leaders, and the clergy gave it their best thought and effort. About 1817, Sunday-schools were

SECOND PERIOD—TRANSITION

generally established. A few churches had them earlier. It is evident that the first half of the nineteenth century was fermenting with religious forces. New wine was bursting the old bottles. New leaders and new methods were called for, and pastors were aroused to their utmost endeavor. Even the consecrated men who sought to hold by the old things were carried off their feet by the inrush of new forces.

The times were of necessity characterized by instability in the pastoral office. Litchfield County abounded in pastors of large ability fitted to lead in a large way. The outside demand for such men was great, and they could not be retained in their parishes. Dr. Bellamy, though the greatest preacher of his day, had been able to stay in his pastorate at Bethlehem for a lifetime. In the new age such men were called to a work in larger communities with an urgency they could not resist. His successor, Dr. Azel Backus, accepted in 1813 the presidency of Hamilton College. Dr. Edward Dorr Griffin, born at East Haddam in 1770, graduated at Yale in 1790, pastor in New Hartford from 1795 to 1801, was called to Newark, New Jersey, and afterward became president of Williams College. Ebenezer Porter, D.D., was born at Cornwall, Connecticut, October 5, 1772, and graduated at Dartmouth in 1792. He was pastor at Washington, Connecticut, from 1796 to 1812, and was called to the professorship of sacred

THE CLERGY OF LITCHFIELD COUNTY

rhetoric in Andover Theological Seminary. He was a man of great intellectual strength and ability, who exercised a wide influence. Dr. Lyman Beecher, after his sixteen years in Litchfield, was called to Boston. He was afterward professor and president of Lane Theological Seminary, Cincinnati. Noah Porter, D.D., LL.D., was pastor at New Milford from 1836 to 1843, afterward professor and president of Yale College. George Pierce, pastor at Harwinton from 1822 to 1834, was called to the presidency of Western Reserve College.

Jonathan Edwards, D.D., pastor at Colebrook from 1796 to 1799, became president of Union College. Ralph Emerson, D.D., the second pastor at Norfolk, and ministering there from 1815 to 1829, was called to a professorship in the theological seminary at Andover, where he filled the chair of history and pastoral theology for twenty-five years with great power and usefulness. He had previously been invited to the presidency of Western Reserve College, but had declined.

The Rev. Harvey D. Kitchell, pastor at Thomaston from 1838 to 1848, after pastorates in Detroit and Chicago became president of Middlebury College. These names selected from many indicate that while Litchfield County in this period had no lack of great men, it had become more difficult to retain them for a life service. It had become easier for both ministers

SECOND PERIOD—TRANSITION

and people to come and go, and if there were inducements for young ministers to come, there were still greater inducements for ministers of established reputations to enter larger fields of work elsewhere. Thus pastors in Litchfield County were called to a much more strenuous and varied work than in the earlier time, were compelled to be leaders in the teaching of new thought and the organizing of new methods, and their time for impressing themselves on the community was short. They became great quickeners of thinking and instigators of change rather than builders of the permanent elements of parish life. It seems to me that they did their work on the whole remarkably well. Rolling stones are not good at gathering moss nor building foundations, but they may accomplish something in other ways. Certainly the ministers of short pastorate and great activity, who, amid controversies, disintegrations, and reorganizations, had charge of the churches in this county from 1800 to 1860, were many of them exceedingly capable men and did well the work given them to do. They developed latent forces in the churches and set their people at work. A sense of responsibility for things was pressed home upon men, women, and children. The separateness and dignity and official authority of the clergy for the most part passed away, but they became leaders in the things that concern the daily life of men.

THE CLERGY OF LITCHFIELD COUNTY

They ceased to begin their preaching from God as a Being wholly known, deducing by logical inference the duty and destiny of men. They began with men in human affairs living under earthly conditions, and tried to lead their people step by step toward God as the great consummation of our human life. Leveling influences were everywhere at work, and as the ministers themselves came down from their high pulpits to the platform nearer their congregation, they taught their fellow-Christians also to become a leaven in human society, even at the risk of soiling their white robes by contact with the dirty work of the world. There was a new world coming rapidly into existence, and with more or less clearness of vision the spiritual guides and teachers recognized the fact, and sought so to make Christianity the center of every movement that it might be the new world wherein shall dwell righteousness. After the storm of theological and ecclesiastical controversy the air became clearer and the essentials of Christian love and brotherly coöperation became apparent to most minds.

The equal rights of men of all opinions and all denominations to a part in the common service of the one Master and Saviour in every community were practically established, though the principles and methods of adjustment, and the achievement of mutual confidence and brotherly confederation, had yet to be thought out. Except in the separation of church and state, which was

SECOND PERIOD—TRANSITION

taken in hand largely by the outside people, the clergy were leaders in every change and readjustment, and the general wisdom shown by them was only emphasized by the exceptional action or adverse criticisms of a few. There were mistakes that wrought injury and left the scars of battle, but, on the whole, the record of ministers and their work was one to be admired and approved by every close and clear-eyed student of this historic period.

CHAPTER VII

PERSONAL SKETCHES

REV. STANLEY GRISWOLD

ERETICS are usually interesting, and in these later days heresy often seems a ground of popularity in a minister. It was a less comfortable thing to differ from one's brethren a century ago. The Rev. Stanley Griswold was an early example of such difference in this county. He was born in Torringford, November 14, 1763, and was graduated from Yale in 1786. He was ordained as pastor in New Milford January 20, 1790, and dismissed in 1802.

Early in his ministry it began to be suspected that he was unsound and unsafe in his theology, but evidently he had no intention of controverting the essentials of the generally accepted belief. I have seen a letter writ-

Congregational Church, Goshen

ten to his father in which he resented the suspicion that he was departing from the faith of the fathers. He was only trying to make that faith workable by using common sense in its application.

From two published sermons on the death of his predecessor, the Rev. Nathaniel Taylor, in 1800, it is easy to see that the standpoint of his thinking and teaching was different from that generally prevalent in his time. He evidently believed that *goodness* was something to be achieved by human choice and effort, and that it gave one a clear title to heaven. He says: "The art, my hearers, of turning death into a pleasing scene, is the most important art ever learned by mortals. Such an art does really exist. We are dull indeed to learn it. Yet it is the most simple art; it consists only in being good. And to be good is far easier than to be evil; for the way of transgressors is hard, whereas the yoke of Christ is easy and his burden light."

Almost any minister of his time would have explained that no hope could be founded on human choice and human goodness, only on the election and grace of God, which must give to our lives their value.

In the second sermon he makes a statement almost equally startling in regard to the nature of rewards and punishments: "Happiness belongs only to the good mind; malice is a hell to its possessor. . . . Sin murders the soul itself, and in the future world anguish and tor-

THE CLERGY OF LITCHFIELD COUNTY

ment assail the foul spirit to a degree inconceivable and unspeakable. Our Saviour speaks of it under the figure of torment occasioned by fire and brimstone, and characterizes it by weeping, wailing, and gnashing of teeth."

Mr. Griswold was a speaker of marked ability, and his church sympathized with him when neighboring ministers objected to his course. He was evidently a man whose character and personal qualities commanded admiration and respect. How far the teaching of his predecessor, Mr. Taylor, prepared the way for his influence, I have no means of knowing, but apparently the old pastor was on the best of terms with the new. In the funeral discourse, Mr. Taylor is said to have held metaphysics "as very unprofitable to be introduced into public discourses," also to have believed some of the heathen might be saved, and to have baptized children "on their own account." The question arises, but cannot be answered by any knowledge in my possession, concerning the influence both of the grandfather and of Mr. Griswold on the career of the young Nathaniel W. Taylor, who was afterward the great exponent of the New Haven theology.

Perhaps Mr. Griswold might have continued in his pastorate but for his prominence in political matters, in which, unlike his brother ministers, he took the side of Jefferson, whose election was regarded by religious leaders in Connecticut as a horrible calamity and a triumph

PERSONAL SKETCHES

of infidelity. In 1803 Mr. Griswold acknowledged such a change of belief that he retired from the ministry. He was afterward United States Senator from Ohio, and Chief Judge of the Northwest Territory. He continued to be a man of religious faith and influence outside the ministry.

REV. ALEXANDER GILLETT

THE REV. ALEXANDER GILLETT was born August 14, 1749, in Granby, Connecticut, "and was the son of pious parents." He was graduated at Yale in 1770, and studied theology under the direction of the Rev. Timothy Pitkin of Farmington. He was pastor at Wolcott, Connecticut, from 1773 to 1791, and of the First Church in Torrington from 1792 until his death in 1826. He frequently aided other pastors in revival services, and had several revivals in his own parish. He made missionary tours in the new settlements of Vermont, leaving his own pulpit for a time to be supplied, and was zealous in holding neighborhood services in the school-houses or in pastoral visiting. His surviving parishioners remembered him with great affection and respect and no unpleasant recollections. It is said by Mr. Orcutt in his "History of Torrington": "He was

THE CLERGY OF LITCHFIELD COUNTY

always seen on Sunday morning coming to church on foot with umbrella and overcoat, the latter on his arm in all weathers, no matter how high the thermometer. Having preached the morning sermon, he frequently closed with the remark, 'Having thus attended to the doctrines of the text, we will consider the applications this afternoon,' and the morning and afternoon sermons were nearly always connected. . . . He was a composer of poetry and music as well as sermons."

His neighbor, the Rev. Frederick Marsh, says of Mr. Gillett: "He was rather above the medium stature and size, of a full habit, broad shoulders, short neck, and large head. . . . His face was broad and unusually square and full, illuminated by large, prominent eyes, the whole indicating more of intellect than of vivacity. He was courteous and kind, swift to hear and slow to speak. . . . As a man of intellectual ability he held a decidedly high rank. He had an aversion to everything superficial. He was an admirable linguist, and above all excelled in the knowledge of the Bible, not merely in his own language but in the original. I have heard an eminent minister, who fitted for college under his instructions, say that he never found any tutor so accurate and thorough in the languages as Mr. Gillett. He was also very familiar and extensively acquainted with history; and he studied history especially as an exposition

PERSONAL SKETCHES

of prophecy. . . . During seventeen years of familiar intercourse with him, my mind became constantly more impressed with the depth of his piety, his unreserved consecration to God, his self-sacrificing devotion to the cause of Christ and the highest interests of his fellowmen. . . . He presented truth with great clearness and point, hence his preaching took strong hold on congregations in the time of revivals. . . . His delivery was rendered laborious and difficult by an impediment in his speech. He could not be called a popular preacher, but he was a skilful and faithful guide to souls, and his labors were abundantly blessed."

Dr. McEwen tells us: "Whatever of management and labor pertained to the farm, he gave exclusively to the family. One large chamber he made his sanctum. It was accommodated with a large old-fashioned fireplace. In this every morning, even through dog days, he made a blazing fire, raising the windows when necessary. His philosophy was that in hot weather a fire in the morning purified the air and by increasing the circulation made it cooler. Few ministers spent more hours in their study than Mr. Gillett." In that room he studied, wrote sermons, poetry, and music, played on the bass viol, and practised for diversion the art of a bookbinder. He is said to have taken up the study of Hebrew and made himself proficient in it after he was

[79]

forty. Perhaps his friends were not the best judges as to what constituted proficiency in Hebrew. One son, Timothy P. Gillett, was a minister and pastor for fifty-one years of the church in Branford, Connecticut.

REV. ASAHEL HOOKER

THE REV. ASAHEL HOOKER was born in Bethlehem, Connecticut, August 29, 1762, in the fifth generation from the Rev. Thomas Hooker, first pastor of Hartford. He was graduated at Yale in 1789, studied theology under the Rev. William Robinson of Southington, Connecticut, and was ordained pastor at Goshen in 1791. Under his ministry the church, which had been in a distracted and divided condition, soon became united and strong.

He took up for a time the work of training theological students, in which he was very successful. He was dismissed in 1810, on account of the failure of his health. He preached afterward with acceptance in New Haven, New York, and Charleston, South Carolina, but did not recover his health fully and died in 1813. His son, Edward W. Hooker, D.D., was a professor at the East Windsor Theological Seminary, and he had grandsons in the ministry. President Heman Humphrey, one of his students, says of him: "He was a good man, of ex-

PERSONAL SKETCHES

cellent talent and high professional acquirements, a devoted pastor, an edifying and a searching preacher, a wise counselor, an earnest defender of the faith once delivered to the saints, an Elisha among the young prophets, a revered and beloved teacher who will ever live in the grateful memory of his pupils as long as any of them survive."

He had lived under the preaching of Dr. Bellamy, with whose doctrinal position he considered himself in essential agreement. I have used one of his sermons, with one of Dr. Bellamy's, in preparing a sample eighteenth-century sermon. He was for several years registrar of both the North Consociation and the Association of Litchfield County, and his records show that ex-President Roosevelt was not the inventor of simplified spelling. We are frequently informed that certain votes were *past,* or that the ecclesiastical body concerned *past* a given vote.

REV. LUTHER HART

THE REV. LUTHER HART was born in Goshen, July 27, 1783, and graduated at Yale in 1807. He studied theology with Dr. Porter of Washington and Mr. Hooker of Goshen. He was ordained pastor in Plymouth, Connecticut, in 1810, and continued in office until he died, April 25, 1834. He was a man greatly beloved by his people and highly honored among his brethren in the ministry. "There was no resisting his candor and manly sincerity, which gave evidence not only of his Christian principle, but of the frankness and honesty of his heart." He was a lover of poetry and music, a writer of poetry, and a musician of high order.

The Rev. Lauren P. Hickok, D.D., says of Mr. Hart: "One of his marked characteristics was an indescribable expression of cheerfulness and hearty good will, diffusing its sweet savor wherever he was, so that his presence and society were always sought. His intercourse with his church and people was very frank and familiar, yet with a large amount of reserved dignity and seriousness. His sermons were serious, pungent, and discriminating, and abounded less in long-drawn argument than in condensed, sententious thoughts and concise declarations. His voice was full and melodious." He had a high reputation for eloquence in the pulpit.

REV. SAMUEL R. ANDREW

THE REV. SAMUEL R. ANDREW was born at Milford, Connecticut, in 1787, and was graduated from Yale in 1807. He was the grandson of the Rev. Samuel Andrew of Milford, Connecticut, who was one of the

PERSONAL SKETCHES

founders of Yale College, and pastor at Milford for fifty years. Mr. Andrew was ordained pastor at Woodbury in 1817 and continued in his pastorate until 1846. He was chosen a member of the Yale Corporation in 1837. "Mr. Andrew's intellect was strong, clear, comprehensive, and discriminating. His judgment was preeminently sound and wise. His taste was pure and classical. His sensibilities were exquisitely susceptible to beauty in nature, in literature, and in character. His thoughts were always just, often rich and original. He was a laborious student, a close, independent, and comprehensive thinker in theology. His sympathies were as tender as his intellect was strong. . . . His piety was the very beauty of holiness, it was so unaffected, so symmetrical, so honest, and so tender. . . . He was strong in faith, giving glory to God; when dreadful waves of sorrow broke over him, he cast himself upon the promises of his covenant God with the simplicity and confidence of a child."[1] His death was sudden and quiet, and he passed away as one greatly loved and lamented.

REV. JAMES BEACH

THE REV. JAMES BEACH was born in Winchester, June 10, 1780, was graduated at Williams College, studied

[1] *New York Observer*, quoted in Cothren's "History of Woodbury."

THE CLERGY OF LITCHFIELD COUNTY

theology with the Rev. Asahel Hooker of Goshen, was ordained pastor of the First Church in Winsted, January 1, 1806, and dismissed January 26, 1842, after a pastorate of thirty-six years. The Rev. Cyrus Yale says of him: "He held a high position among his clerical brethren, was one whom they delighted to honor, and this the more the older he grew and the better they knew him. His great weight of character and rare influence seemed to result very much from a happy combination of deep piety, cultivated and vigorous intellect, sterling sense, uniform judiciousness, joined to his marked sobriety, his brotherly kindness, and his dignified manner, his steady manifestation of strong love to God and of God's truths as he saw them on the sacred page in lines of light and glory. How all desired to have him lead in devotional exercises on all occasions as one preeminently endowed with the gift and the grace of prayer!
. . . The person of Mr. Beach, though not tall, was commanding, his eyes deep set beneath heavy brows. . . . He was singularly well formed for strength of body and of mind, gravity and goodness had about equal possession of his countenance, while reason was more strongly developed than imagination."

Dr. Joseph Eldridge says of Mr. Beach: "His disposition was social and genial. He was a pleasant man to meet. He had a considerate regard for his ministerial brethren in respect to their feelings and reputa-

PERSONAL SKETCHES

tions, rejoiced in their successes and their usefulness. I never saw him out of temper, never heard him utter a harsh or censorious remark. He never thrust himself forward, but was more disposed to stand back and make room for others. His sermons were full of truth clearly and plainly expressed. In their delivery he was earnest but never impassioned; perhaps more animation would have improved them. His prayers in public, especially those on special occasions, were very remarkable for their ease, their felicitous adaptations in all respects to the circumstances of the case, and the happy introduction of scriptural quotations, and at the same time remarkable for their exemption from everything in the nature of effort and display, and for their simple tone and humble contrition." He died in Winsted on his birthday, June 10, 1850, seventy years of age.

REV. CHAUNCEY LEE, D.D.

THE REV. CHAUNCEY LEE, D.D., a son of the Rev. Jonathan Lee, was born in Salisbury, Connecticut, in 1763, and was graduated at Yale in 1784. He was pastor at Sunderland, Vermont, from 1790 to 1797. He became pastor in Colebrook, Connecticut, in February, 1800, and continued in office there until January, 1828. He died in Hartwick, New York, in 1842. His son, the

THE CLERGY OF LITCHFIELD COUNTY

Rev. Chauncey G. Lee, was pastor at Monroe, Connecticut, from 1821 to 1826, and afterward in other Connecticut churches. His grandson, the Rev. Clarence Beebe, was a missionary in Turkey. I used to hear Deacon Abel S. Wetmore of Winchester speak of Dr. Lee from personal remembrance, while his published books and local traditions show him to be a man of too much importance to pass by without notice.

He began authorship with a new decimal arithmetic which Thomas Robbins, in the mature judgment of eighteen years, pronounces "pedantic." I do not know of any copy now in use. In 1806 he published a translation of the Book of Job in the form of an epic poem entitled "The Trial of Virtue." The influence of Milton is manifest in his style. The book had considerable popularity, and is creditable both for its scholarship and its poetic expression. He was an evangelist of marked success, and in 1824 published a volume of sermons forming a system of preaching for revival purposes. This series of sermons was accompanied by a collection of hymns, composed by Dr. Lee himself, to reinforce the impression of the preaching. Sermons and hymns alike seem to have been well adapted to this purpose. Deacon Wetmore, whose own religious experience had been vitally affected by Dr. Lee's preaching, used to repeat to me sentence after sentence from a sermon which he had heard as a young man. The language was

PERSONAL SKETCHES

remarkably clear and impressive and could hardly have failed to be clearly understood by any congregation. Outside the pulpit Dr. Lee was irrepressibly humorous, but the sermons gave no indication of it. His wife was said to have made the remark that when she saw him outside the pulpit she often thought he ought never to go into it, and that when she listened to him in the pulpit, it seemed as if he ought to stay there always. We read in Sprague's "Annals": "On one public occasion, at the dinner-table, where there was a large company, he indulged his passion for humor to such extent as to produce long-continued and convulsive laughter. When Mr. Lathrop of Salisbury said afterward, in a tone of solemnity, 'I think we have been indebted to you for much amusement,' his countenance fell, and he said, 'Well, my dear brother, I am sorry, I am sorry; if I have done wrong I hope God will forgive me.'"

I will venture on a quotation from "The Trial of Virtue":

> My friends, deceitful as th' inconstant brook,
> With smiling fortune smil'd: with it forsook
> The limpid stream, by winter's frost congealed,
> Spread to the eye a smooth delightful field;
> Firm to the foot, not rocks more firm and fast,
> And dreaming fancy thought the scene would last.
> But short th' illusion,—ere one summer's day,
> The charm is fled, the ice dissolves away,

THE CLERGY OF LITCHFIELD COUNTY

The waters swiftly glide, the dream is o'er,
The rivulet dries, and friendship is no more.
Hope, fair deceiver, downward to the deep,
Floats with the tide and leaves the wretch to weep.

REV. FREDERICK MARSH

THE REV. FREDERICK MARSH was born in New Hartford, September 18, 1780. He prepared for college with Mr. Robbins of Norfolk, graduated at Yale in 1805, studied theology under Dr. Hooker of Goshen, preached in Winchester from the beginning of 1808, where he was ordained pastor February 1, 1809, and continued in active service until February 1, 1846. He continued to live in Winchester until his death in February, 1873, preaching occasionally in near-by places.

His early manhood, spent under the pastorate of Dr. Edward Dorr Griffin, determined his religious experience and his theological belief. Dr. Griffin was always his ideal. What Dr. Griffin had preached was to him the eternal and unchangeable truth of God. He was modest, cautious, painfully conscientious, a pastor of firm and enduring faithfulness; he took life seriously, and, according to tradition, was never known but once to make a facetious remark accompanied by a smile. In the revivals under his ministry his one fear was that he should encourage some inquirer to indulge in a false

Frederick Marsh

PERSONAL SKETCHES

hope and think himself a Christian without becoming such in reality. Knowing that the whole matter was in the hands of God and had been settled from before the foundation of the world, it would seem a little inconsistent, not to say cruel, that the deluded person might not be permitted a little comfort here before facing the eternal reality. But Mr. Marsh did not look at it in that way. It is said that the death of a child in early infancy was the cause of a long period of deep melancholy, as he could find no solid evidence of the child's salvation, and was greatly burdened at the possibility that he was responsible for the coming into being of one who was to be the heir of endless torment, without even the opportunity of a personal choice in the matter. The question was discussed at length before a ministers' club of that day of which Mr. Marsh was a member: "Will those who die in infancy be saved?" "After a full discussion the meeting was agreed that probably some who die in infancy are saved." The meeting was held in Plymouth, May 31, 1814. The careful conclusion of these good men does not seem to have brought the comfort to his burdened heart that we might think it ought to have done.

Mr. Marsh was an expert penman, and usually had charge of the records of Association or Consociation in his day. It is a pleasure to read any records made by his hand. His tastes were historic and he furnished valuable manuscript material to the Connecticut Historical Society, which has been preserved in their library at Hartford. In the beginning of my ministry in Winchester, Mr. Marsh was usually present in the Sunday congregation. His appearance was saintly beyond that of any other person in my memory. His presence was of itself a sermon and a benediction. Dr. Eldridge of Norfolk once said of him: "His influence over his brethren was silent, modest, not obtrusive; not so much that of great intellectual power as of sincerity, truth, self-sacrifice, and unfeigned devotion. No jealousy in his mind of his brethren, if they had gifts; no jealousy of their reputation, if they acquired it; no jealousy of their influence, but delighted by it wherever it was manifesting itself."

When he passed away in his ninety-third year he left behind him an influence that will not perish through the ages. It is worth while for any community to secure the lifelong presence of such a man. Though his theology may pass away, his Christian manhood is a triumph of faith, the value of which will endure through all changes.

As the new pastor, I was always treated by Mr. Marsh with the utmost kindness and confidence. Judging by his countenance, my preaching was often a puzzle to him, but never except on a single occasion did I meet

PERSONAL SKETCHES

with the slightest expression of dissent or reproof on his part. Knowing that he had passed through several great revivals, I once asked him what he thought the best time of year to plan for evangelistic work in the parish. A look of pain came upon his face as if he had been listening to blasphemy, and he replied solemnly, "When God sends a revival, is the time for a revival." He believed in revivals, and by his own report six sevenths of those whom he received to the church came into the Christian life through revivals, but he neither planned for revivals nor undertook to produce them. They came in answer to prayer and long waiting upon God. It was his part to apply careful tests that the genuineness of God's working might be assured; to be careful to suppress tendencies to excitement or disorder; and to prevent too easy or careless acceptance of the Christian hope on the part of the converts. In 1821, after several months of deep feeling and anxiety among his young people, he organized with much hesitation a young people's meeting for their help and guidance, which on the whole he regarded as having beneficial results.

Judging from the characteristics of his descendants, connected with occasional incidents related of himself, I cannot regard him as having been destitute of humor. The one joke remembered of him was that, once going into a room where the ladies of the parish were gathered

THE CLERGY OF LITCHFIELD COUNTY

and evidently enjoying themselves, he told them of an ancient scholar who had discovered Scripture proof that there were no women in heaven, quoting from the eighth chapter of the Revelation: "There was silence in heaven for about the space of half an hour." His restraint was largely due to his interpretation of the saying of Jesus, "For every idle word that men shall speak they shall give account in the day of judgment." He evidently regarded it as a condemnation of careless talking, while we of this day only read it as a statement of the completeness and minuteness of the judgment of God, which misses no detail of our lives.

As an illustration of his method with converts, and of the type of religious experience looked for in those days, I will quote in condensed form an account of the conversion of his son, a deaf-and-dumb boy of seventeen years, as it was written by Mr. Marsh, and published in the *Connecticut Evangelical Magazine* for October, 1832. This son, Jonathan, had learned to read and write and use the sign-language, and was remarkably intelligent, but the father found it hard to be sure that he understood things of a spiritual order. There was a revival in the fall of 1831, and for a week or two he had shown deep anxiety.

"On Sabbath evening, October 2d, when he was more particularly conversed with, and urged to immediate repentance, he became deeply impressed. He wept for his sins and prayed to God. On Monday morning he retired to a grove for an hour or two, and then to the barn, where he spent the day fasting; and it was near night before he could be persuaded to come into the house. 'Tuesday' (he says) 'I felt very sorry, for my hard heart was hard to repent.' He spent four days in retirement with his Bible. Often would he come with his slate with questions like these: 'How shall I repent? My heart is hard. It will not repent. I am wretched and unhappy. I wish to repent sincerely. How shall I?' Deep solemnity and distress were settled upon his countenance, and we hardly dared say anything to him lest we should make some wrong impression upon his mind."

About noon on Friday "he came to me with the questions, 'Will God do no more? Is it easy to repent?' He was told that none but God could help him. As it stood upon his slate, this remark arrested his attention remarkably, and with his mind intensely fixed upon it, he retired to his room. I feared to say one word. In the distant part of the house his groans were heard. On opening the door, I found him walking the room, his face suffused with tears. He took little notice of any one, and asked no more questions, but seemed to feel that the controversy was between God and his own soul. At evening he appeared calm and apparently cheerful. On being asked how he felt, he replied,

THE CLERGY OF LITCHFIELD COUNTY

'Happy a little.' From answers to various questions that were put to him the next day, we began to cherish a trembling hope that through riches of infinite mercy he had been brought to the foot of the cross, and that the Holy Spirit had taken away the stony heart and given a heart of flesh. Nothing was said about hope, or that would lead him to think we supposed there was any saving change. Saturday evening his countenance beamed the peace that dwelt in his soul. To the question, 'Do you feel more careless about religion than you did yesterday?' he replied, 'I feel more proper, and think that it is a precious religion.' He seemed almost in ecstasies while reading the stanza beginning with 'How sweet the name of Jesus sounds.' He looked about with tears in his eyes, and expressed his surprise that he had not loved God before, it was so easy and God was so good. Yet he often said, 'I think I love God all, but I fear my heart is deceitful.' "

This trembling hope seems to have been about as far as Mr. Marsh thought it safe to go in religious experience. It was about the utmost that he dared to go in the expression of his own personal faith, until a few weeks before his death.

CHAPTER VIII

THIRD PERIOD—MODERNISM

ROM about 1860 the churches and ministers in Litchfield County entered upon a third period of development. They could no longer keep to themselves, for the great current of the world's life swept over and about them with ever-increasing force. The growth of villages along the railroads brought an influx of new inhabitants from many lands. Foreign-born people occupied the farms left behind by men of the old New England stock. Dwellers in the cities were drawn by the purity of the air and the beauty of the landscape to find a summer home among the hills. All these people brought with them their own religious, or irreligious, ideals and customs. The earlier war between Calvinists and Arminians, or old school and new school, was outworn and only remembered or understood by a

THE CLERGY OF LITCHFIELD COUNTY

few veterans. It was no longer a question of Congregationalist, Episcopalian, Baptist, or Methodist. The Roman Catholics were present in multitudes. Preaching was called for in French, German, Swedish, and Italian. The negro population insisted on churches of their own.

The utmost freedom of theological thinking, and the largest variety in ritual and method of worship, came to be conceded as an unquestioned right. The whole trend of preaching and pastoral service was toward coöperation, with the thought of federation becoming ever more prominent. The habit and training of the older churches still called for men of ability and capacity for leadership in their pulpits. The newer churches of all denominations could not choose but make the same demand.

I do not plan to speak of living men, but I am aware of no deterioration in the character and standing of the Litchfield County pulpit. There were men of the past who stood out with a prominence to which we can furnish no parallel to-day. There is a closeness of association with the outside world which often promotes a more rapid change of pastorate. There is an interchange of persons and of influence which prevents Litchfield County from standing out with the separateness of identity which characterized much of her past history. Her children are in other places, leavening the

THIRD PERIOD—MODERNISM

life and thought of the nation, but we are not prepared to admit any signs of decadence in her churches, nor in the men who occupy her pulpits.

Changes have been great in methods of preparing sermons, in the multiplicity of themes selected for preaching, and in the freedom of Biblical interpretation, or the following out of personal tastes in the presentation of the Gospel. Differences of belief, and liberty in the expression of those differences, are accepted without rancor or bitterness. The minister is recognized as a leader if he is fitted to lead, and his message is listened to with respect, but his old-time official authority is no longer recognized. The people have come into their inheritance and exercise a right of thinking and acting for themselves, whoever may be chosen as their teacher and guide.

There is a kind of difference in the churches unknown to the earlier times. When all communities consisted of a homogeneous farming population, with here and there a man conspicuous for wealth or social rank, each parish might have its local pride and might develop peculiarities, but the churches were on a practical equality in financial standing and in their provision for support of their ministers. In these later days many rural parishes have fallen off greatly in population and in financial ability; besides, heterogeneous and unassimilated elements prevent the social unity of

THE CLERGY OF LITCHFIELD COUNTY

other days. Salaries of the clergy have in many cases been greatly, sometimes painfully, reduced.

Over against this fact, wealth has greatly increased in neighboring villages, and their churches are able to offer comparatively large salaries. The financial gain combined with the larger opportunity offers to ministers of ability an inducement which may clearly mean duty. Hence the clergy no longer stand on an equal footing in regard to the development and maintenance of either personal or official influence. None the less it is my firm conviction that even under the least favorable conditions the clergy of this county still have an opportunity for the higher manhood that no worldly wealth can measure.

CHAPTER IX

MORE PERSONAL SKETCHES

REV. JOSEPH ELDRIDGE, D.D.

HE great man of my early ministry was Dr. Joseph Eldridge of Norfolk, and the many years that have since passed by have taken away nothing from my belief in his greatness. He was not the only great man or great minister in the history of Norfolk, but the beneficent impress of his influence in that town and in Litchfield County is something we cannot afford to forget.

The Rev. Joseph Eldridge, D.D., was born in Yarmouth, Massachusetts, July 8, 1804, graduated at Yale in 1829, was installed pastor at Norfolk April 25, 1832, resigned his pastorate November 1, 1874, and died March 31, 1875.

THE CLERGY OF LITCHFIELD COUNTY

He did not impress one as a student of the academic sort, intrenched in learned subtleties, nor did he prepare orations which displayed eloquence or grandeur of diction. He was a man of large mind and extensive information, but his greatness seemed most of all due to his large-heartedness. He had a ready grasp of practical questions because of his deep interest in everything that affected the welfare of men and women. He loved his kind and studied humanity, not as a scientific problem, but as a means of understanding and helping the living, concrete persons whom he saw on every side in need of personal sympathy. It was a matter of course that the younger ministers went to him for advice and assistance in their difficulties. They knew he loved them and understood them, and that he had a comprehensive grasp of the problems that perplexed them. The utter simplicity and sincerity of the man went straight to the root of all practical questions. He saw at once the thing that was just and kind, and insisted that only that should be done, and done at once. Anything oppressive or unfair or lacking in brotherly kindness aroused his indignation, and he had an intense power of indignation. Flippancy and irreverence brought instant reproof, but the common frailties and failures of his brethren met with his ready forbearance, and his sympathy was available in every trouble. He seldom failed to be present at meetings of the ministers

Joseph Eldridge

MORE PERSONAL SKETCHES

or churches, and was easily first in every gathering, though seemingly the only person unconscious of the fact. Many of the younger pastors learned from him ministerial secrets of great value. I will mention but one nugget of advice which has many times recurred to my memory. It was that if ever I felt called upon to preach the wrath of God, I should do it conscientiously and thoroughly, but tenderly, not mixing any of my own wrath with it; to feel sure in such case that "the wrath of man worketh not the righteousness of God."

The commemoration sermon by Dr. Noah Porter, President of Yale, gives a fuller outline of the man and his work than could have place in these sketches, but I feel it necessary to express my own sense of his great worth. All who knew him had a high ideal of Christian manhood put before them.

REV. ADAM REID, D.D.

THE REV. ADAM REID, D.D., was born in Wishaw, Lanarkshire, Scotland, January 4, 1808. He was graduated at Glasgow University in 1827, was Trustee of Williams College from 1847 to 1869, and received the degree of D.D. from Union College in 1854.

THE CLERGY OF LITCHFIELD COUNTY

He began preaching in Salisbury, Connecticut, November, 1836, was ordained pastor in September, 1837, resigned his work in September, 1877, after forty-one years of service, and died of apoplexy November 2, 1878, at the age of nearly seventy-one years.

He was renowned for ability and eloquence, and quite early in his pastorate received calls to Rochester, Baltimore, Providence, New York, Hartford, and Boston. His work was mainly in his study and in his pulpit. It has been said that he never repeated sermons, and always had new sermons written ahead for future emergencies, so that at the time of his resignation he had about forty manuscript sermons on hand which had never been used, and that he continued writing new ones from habit up to the time of his death. In his later years, at least, he seemed exceedingly shy, and seldom attended gatherings of ministers or churches outside his parish, although great effort was made to secure his presence. He invariably declined to preach at ordination or installation services, or at meetings of the association to which he belonged. Dr. Eldridge could sometimes get him to a meeting at Norfolk, when at the dinner-table he shone with brilliancy, but it was impossible to draw him out in the public meetings where free discussion was going on.

I have sat by his side on such occasions, when his interest in everything said was intense. He overflowed

MORE PERSONAL SKETCHES

in private suggestions with regard to questions he wanted asked or points to be urged, but would not personally enter the debate. It was said of him by a friend of his earlier days: "He spake as one overmastered by the truth he was setting forth, and thinking not of himself, but of the message he was bearing. He had the power of clothing the simplest truths in forms of beauty and majesty, and his delivery was singularly impressive from the deep earnestness which characterized it. His whole frame quivered with emotion, and the tones of his voice stirred and thrilled the very depths of the heart. His whispers were audible to the farthest parts of the house, and touched and subdued the spirit beyond the loudest declamation." In his farewell sermon he expressed his belief that no pastorate had ever been more peaceful than his, absolutely no jars, quarrels, or difficulties, but perfect sympathy between pastor and people.

REV. LAVALETTE PERRIN, D.D.

THE REV. LAVALETTE PERRIN, D.D., was born in Vernon, Connecticut, May 15, 1816, and graduated at Yale in 1840. He was ordained pastor at Goshen, Connecticut, in 1843, and dismissed September 4, 1857. After a pastorate of twelve years in New Britain, he returned to Litchfield County, and was pastor of the Third Church in Torrington from July 1, 1872, until his death in 1889.

Yale gave him the degree of D.D. in 1869, and he was a member of the Corporation from 1882. He was Treasurer of the National Council from 1880, and Annalist of the Connecticut Conference from 1876. He was a man of fine personal appearance and impressive manner, with conservative tastes and a great liking for systematic and orderly methods. Given to large enthusiasms, his culture and training kept his powers under perfect control; while he gained his ends by patience and persistence, his action was always marked by due caution and judicious balance. It was largely through his influence that the General Conference of the Congregational Churches of Connecticut was organized in 1867. His zeal for the closer and more effective union of the churches led him also to secure the establishment at Hartford of a Memorial Hall to be a recognized center for the official life and activity of Congregationalism in the State. He was instrumental in raising the fund for this purpose. His desire to give the same churches an organ for promoting closer acquaintance and fellowship led him to become editor of the *Religious Herald* from 1876 to 1881.

In every way he was a power for good, not only in the churches of which he was pastor, but widely in the

Lavalette Perrin

MORE PERSONAL SKETCHES

State and country. His work was always constructive and eminently judicious. He planted no seeds of trouble or division. He was a model in the drawing up of statements or resolutions for the action of councils in cases where there were elements of faction or ill feeling. He could fittingly call attention to everything that was good or pleasant on either side, and give the utmost credit that honesty would allow, while quietly minimizing the unpleasant things by suggesting a larger point of view. He will long be remembered with affection and gratitude by many in the churches of Litchfield County, and by some with ardent admiration and enthusiasm as representing just what a pastor should be. He and his wife died together in the Park Hotel disaster at Hartford. One son who survived him is a professor in Yale University.

REV. WILLIAM ELLIOTT BASSETT

ONE of the most interesting and useful men whom it has ever been my privilege to know was the Rev. William E. Bassett, a man for the last eighteen years of his short life intimately connected with the churches of Litchfield County. He was born in Derby, Connecticut, May 24, 1829, graduated from Yale College in 1850, and from Yale Theological Seminary in 1854. After pastorates in Central Village and North Manchester, Connecticut, he was acting pastor and pastor in Warren, Connecticut, from 1863 to 1875, and in Bethlehem, Connecticut, from 1879 to 1881. He preached in North Canaan in 1881, and died at Norfolk November 6, 1881. He was a slender man of medium height, homely in features and awkward in gestures. He was possessed of a wide range of information, and thought deeply on many things, but his interest in life was intensely practical. His sermons were thought out in every detail, were original, fresh, and had a definite practical aim in every part.

After preaching two sermons a week in Warren for twelve years, he resigned because he thought less than two sermons on Sunday demoralizing to the congregation, and he could not repeat his old sermons, each of which had so distinctive a purpose that he felt it would be recognized by former hearers and discounted accordingly. His people were willing to do with one sermon a week, or to hear the old ones over, but he could not be induced to stay when his health seemed insufficient to fulfil his own ideals. He was Registrar of the Litchfield North Association, and a leader in all special work of the churches. When local conferences of the churches were organized to carry out the purpose of the General Conference of Connecticut, Mr. Bassett drew up the constitution. When the inspiration for any new

MORE PERSONAL SKETCHES

thing came from Dr. Joseph Eldridge or Dr. Lavalette Perrin, Mr. Bassett was always depended on to furnish the criticism, draw up the details of the plan, and make it workable. He was indefatigable in making things work, and cheerfully kept himself out of sight behind others, so far as practicable. Many churches and ministers were greatly indebted to him, and some of us found him exceedingly lovable.

REV. HIRAM EDDY, D.D.

HIRAM EDDY was born in Pittsfield, Vermont, March 17, 1813. He attended both Hamilton and Oberlin colleges, and was ordained at Sherman, New York, June 11, 1839. After various pastorates in New York State, he began service at East Canaan, Connecticut, in 1853. He went from his pastorate there to Winsted, Connecticut, where he was installed January 9, 1861, and dismissed October 16, 1865. After pastorates in Milwaukee, Wisconsin, and Jersey City, New Jersey, he returned in 1881 to Canaan, Connecticut, where he died November 30, 1893.

I quote the following description from an address of the Rev. John Calvin Goddard: "As a preacher, Dr. Eddy held a commanding place. He riveted attention

THE CLERGY OF LITCHFIELD COUNTY

from the moment of his appearance. His voice was wide of compass and deep of volume. He could upon occasion roar as a lion robbed of its prey, and again the tones would sink to the power that is not of the whirlwind, nor of the thunder, but of a still small voice. His tread was martial. He could not, like Ahab, go softly before the Lord. He tramped the platform like an armed man. . . . I liked to see him charge the platform from the aisle, his jaw set, his eye fixed, his manner confident, as when Jonathan said to his armor-bearer, 'Come up after me; for the Lord hath delivered them into our hands'; and it was he who left behind him for the men of the pulpit that inspiring utterance, 'It is worth while to have lived, if only for the joy of preaching one true sermon.' "

During his Winsted pastorate, the outbreak of the Civil War led him to go to the front as chaplain of the Second Connecticut Volunteers. He was taken prisoner at the battle of Bull Run, and spent a year in rebel prisons. It is said that his prison experience changed his hair from deep black to white. In the years when I knew him, his gigantic figure, crowned with a halo of bushy hair, pure white, made an impression of personal grandeur and majesty seldom equaled. He was a man of heavenly visions, priest and prophet by temperament and experience.

I wish to quote here from one of his own sermons,

MORE PERSONAL SKETCHES

both as a sample of his style, and as suggestive of the lesson taught by his own closing years:

"The leaf bursts forth into singing when the frost begins to settle on it and the cold winds to shake it. It causes the frost to contribute to its beauty. It uses frosts and storms in the same way and to the same end that it does the sunshine and the summer shower. What a lesson! If you will hold still, the frost will beautify you, the frost of age, the frost of adversity. . . . Wouldst thou have more beauty grow out in thy character? Then let the pinching frosts of affliction and adversity do their work. Wait until the forces are strong enough, and the beauties of grace will show themselves all over thy soul, when through these afflictions the love of Jesus comes, glowing and shining, warming and softening, like the morning flood-lights of heaven. Wait, and the white lilies of purity will bloom in thy heart, and the morning-glories of joy and thankfulness will climb along the corridors of thy soul, and the plants of righteousness shall bloom there in ever-increasing profusion; but, like some natural fruits and beauties, the frost is necessary to this result—patiently wait."

A vision of Jesus Christ dominated and glorified his life.

CHAPTER X

THE EPISCOPAL CHURCH

HE introduction of the Episcopal Church, or, as it was called at first, the Church of England, into what is now the county of Litchfield preceded the organization of the county in 1751. This introduction was especially due to three causes: First, there were many persons coming into this part of the country from England who "at home," as they were accustomed to say, were members of the Church of England, whose love for its services, its customs, its principles, had suffered no diminution from their change of residence. Whatever reasons had moved them to come to this country, they did not come to escape from ecclesiastical burdens, nor with the idea of finding a freedom which had been denied to them in their earlier abode. That which they remembered was not religious tyranny and

THE EPISCOPAL CHURCH

forms of worship as a burden to their conscience, creeds demanding too great an exercise of faith. Their thoughts went back to religious homes where they had been at peace. They felt as the Psalmist did when he cried, "If I forget thee, O Jerusalem, let my right hand forget her cunning." It was natural, then, that as soon as they had settled down to their work of reclaiming the wilderness and had become acquainted with their neighbors, they should seek out those whose sentiments accorded with their own; also that little circles should meet on Sunday morning, in which one of their numbers should read the familiar words of Morning Prayer and Litany, and probably read a printed sermon drawn from the rich treasury of English theology, which treasury has never been lacking in words full of grave wisdom and of comfort for the soul burdened with its sense of weakness and sin, and so the next step was to secure the occasional visit of some clergyman of that church to conduct its services and to administer the sacraments held in such high esteem.

It was in 1740, in the town of Plymouth, that the services of the Church of England were first brought into this county. Three years before, in 1737, nineteen petitioners living in Plymouth, who were accustomed to attend the Congregational Church in Waterbury, desired for themselves the privilege of holding services during three winter months in their own town.

THE CLERGY OF LITCHFIELD COUNTY

The second of the three causes to which the growth of the English Church in this country could be attributed had now begun to be felt. By the middle of the eighteenth century there had been built in the limits of Connecticut fourteen Episcopal churches, and there were perhaps five thousand persons, young and old, who were connected with them. These people felt that the law of the State compelling them to pay taxes for building houses of worship and supporting the clergy of the State religion was a burden. Accordingly, they sought relief from the General Assembly. When, after considerable discussion and delay, they were relieved from this burden, it was found that persons not very strong in their attachment to the Congregational order sought to join the Episcopalians, not out of regard for the principles of that church, but because they were not taxed so heavily. From this probably arose the custom of "certificating off" from the Established Church. Many of these certificates are still in existence and are variously expressed, one reading: "I hereby certify that I have left the Church of God and joined the Episcopalians." It is to be hoped that this man, as was the case with many who thus became identified with the Episcopal Church, found that he was not left in such alienation from the "Mother of us all" as his words might lead us to suppose that he expected to be.

The third cause which may be assigned for the

THE EPISCOPAL CHURCH

growth of the Episcopal Church was the feeling, which widely prevailed, that the preaching of the Rev. Mr. Whitefield, and the excitement created by it, was leading to dangerous extremes. The Rev. George Whitefield, who had been admitted to deacon's orders in the twenty-second year of his age, came to this country, landing at Savannah, in the year 1738. He is said to have drawn multitudes to hear his eloquent sermons. After about four months he returned to England, and although a report had been made that he had followed a somewhat erratic course while in America, and not conformed very closely to the doctrine, discipline, and worship of the church which had given to him his commission, he was admitted to priest's orders. On his second visit to this country, and especially in New England, he put aside all regard for the authority and teaching of the Church of England. At first his eloquence and the spiritual doctrines set forth by him won him a cordial welcome, and it is said that the sermon preached by him when leaving Boston was listened to by twenty thousand people, but under the enthusiasm aroused many adopted his methods and practices who had not his ability. Under their preaching, which soon outran all efforts of civil and ecclesiastical authority to restrain them, much strife and discord were created. There were cases where societies were split and became hostile camps. When Whitefield, two or three years

THE CLERGY OF LITCHFIELD COUNTY

later, proposed to revisit New England, his plan was not well received. A meeting of the Consociation of Congregational Ministers of New Haven County, held in 1745, published a pamphlet disapproving of Whitefield's itineracy, his doctrines—his whole course, in fact. The General Association of Connecticut said it was "needful to declare that if he should make his progress through this Government, it would by no means be advisable for any of their ministers to admit him into their pulpits, or for any of their people to attend his ministrations."

During these disturbances members of the Church of England were strengthened in their attachment to their own church, and found that her sober and spiritual worship was attracting new attention, and a very large number of Congregationalists, distrusting the extravagances and disorders of their day, found in the reverential worship of the Church of England and in the Scriptural character of her doctrines that comfort which seemed to be denied to them elsewhere. By their accession to this church, a new impulse was given to her growth. Indeed, Dr. Johnson of Stratford, writing to a friend in London describing the effect which had been wrought among the people of the State by the disturbances and division to which reference has been made, said: "It has occasioned such a growth of the Church in this town, as well as in many other places, that the church will

THE EPISCOPAL CHURCH

not hold us, and we are obliged to rebuild or else enlarge" (Beardsley's "History of the Episcopal Church in Connecticut," page 133).

BETHLEHEM

THE parish of Christ Church, Bethlehem, was organized in the year 1806, through the agency of the Rev. Dr. Daniel Burhans of Newtown. Services were first held in the Center School-house, but in 1829 a church was built which is still in use. The following clergymen were at different times in charge of the parish: from 1807 to 1814, the Rev. Russell Wheeler; from 1814 to 1816, the Rev. Joseph D. Welton; from 1822 to 1827, the Rev. Sturges Gilbert; in 1828, the Rev. Isaac Jones; in 1830, the Rev. Russell Wheeler; in 1832, the Rev. Joseph Scott; in 1834, the Rev. John Dowdney; from 1835 to 1837, the Rev. William Watson; from 1837 to 1839, the Rev. T. W. Snow; from August, 1839, to Easter, 1844, the Rev. Isaac H. Tuttle; from 1844 to 1847, the Rev. Jonathan Coe; from 1847 to 1848, the Rev. William H. Frisbie; from 1848 to 1851, the Rev. J. S. Covell; in 1852, the Rev. Dr. J. D. Berry; in 1853, the Rev. N. W. Monroe; from 1854 to April, 1855, the Rev. James R. Coe; in 1857, the Rev. Dr. J. D. Berry and the Rev. Edward P. Gray; from 1858

THE CLERGY OF LITCHFIELD COUNTY

to 1861, the Rev. John N. Marvin; from 1861 to August, 1865, the Rev. Dr. Frederick Holcomb; from September, 1865, as lay reader until his ordination in April, 1866, and then until February, 1870, the Rev. A. N. Lewis. The journals of Convention show that no rector was in charge in the years 1870, 1871, and 1872. From 1873 to 1874, the Rev. X. Alanson Welton; from 1878 to 1883, the Rev. James B. Robinson; from 1884 to April, 1890, the Rev. Ralph H. Bowles; from 1890 to July, 1895, the Rev. J. Chauncey Linsley; from 1895 to 1897, the Rev. J. T. Hargrave; from 1898 to 1899, the Rev. Edward M. Skagen; from 1900 to 1903, the Rev. L. Robert Sheffield; from 1903 as lay reader until his ordination in 1906, and then until July, 1907, the Rev. Sidney H. Dixon. At present the parish is without a rector, the Rev. Alexander Hamilton officiating on Sundays.

BRIDGEWATER

THE organization of St. Mark's Church, Bridgewater, dates from April 23, 1810. No church edifice was built before 1835. The church services were held up to that date in private houses by visiting clergymen. Since 1839 the following named persons have served as rectors: from 1839 to 1840, the Rev. Joseph S.

Congregational Church, Salisbury

THE EPISCOPAL CHURCH

Covell; from 1840 to 1841, the Rev. Abel Nichols; from 1841 to 1842, the Rev. Joseph H. Nichols; from 1842 to 1844, the Rev. George S. Gordon; from 1844 to 1846, the Rev. William Atwill; from 1847 to 1850, the Rev. Abel Ogden; from 1852 to 1853, the Rev. Abel Nichols; from 1854 to 1856, the Rev. Merritt H. Wellman; from 1857 to 1859, the Rev. William H. Cook; from 1860 to 1864, the Rev. James Morton; from 1865 to 1868, the Rev. Dr. H. D. Noble; from 1869 to 1871, the Rev. X. Alanson Welton; from 1872 to 1879, the Rev. Dr. W. B. Colburn; from 1880 to 1882, the Rev. Dr. G. V. C. Eastman; from 1885 to 1888, the Rev. William E. Hooker; from 1889 to 1895, the Rev. George Henry Smith; from 1897 to 1898, the Rev. H. L. Everest; from 1898 to 1899, the Rev. A. T. De Learsay; from 1899 to 1902, the Rev. Wilfrid H. Dean; from November 23, 1902, the present rector, the Rev. Gideon D. Pond.

CANAAN

THE parish of Christ Church was organized in the year 1846, and a church building was erected that same year. The Rev. Mr. Fash had charge of the parish at that time. The Rev. George L. Foote, the Rev. William Atwill, the Rev. Mr. Reynolds, the Rev. A. H. Nichols

THE CLERGY OF LITCHFIELD COUNTY

of Salisbury held services in Canaan from the year 1846 to 1850, although none of them was in charge as rector. In 1854 the Rev. H. V. Gardner was rector from Easter, 1854, to Easter, 1855. Then for two years, from 1856 to 1858, the Rev. H. S. Atwater was in charge, officiating every other Sunday. He died December 28, 1879, aged eighty-two years. After him came the Rev. Clayton Eddy, from 1860 to 1861; the Rev. William Williams, 1863; the Rev. H. C. Stowell, 1865. The Rev. Elisha Whittlesey, who for two years was pastor of the Congregational Church, became rector of Christ Church June 25, 1871, and resigned July 15, 1877. The Rev. H. I. Bodley, from July 15, 1877, to March, 1882; the Rev. Francis Barnett, from 1882 to 1899; the Rev. Milton H. Mill, from September 7, 1899, to February 28, 1905. The present rector took charge September 17, 1905.

EAST PLYMOUTH

THE parish known as St. Matthew's, East Plymouth, was first started in 1787. Very little is known of its early history. From 1795 until 1805 it was in the care of the Rev. Alexander Viets Griswold, who afterward became the first bishop of the "Eastern Diocese," which comprised the whole of New England, Connecticut ex-

THE EPISCOPAL CHURCH

cepted. From 1812 to 1817 the Rev. Roger Searle exercised his office here in connection with Plymouth. From 1818 to 1828 the Rev. Rodney Rossiter was in charge; in 1841, the Rev. F. B. Woodward; from 1846 to 1847, the Rev. H. V. Gardner; at Easter, 1848, Collis I. Potter, as lay reader, was in charge until 1850; in 1851-52, the Rev. Dr. Frederick Holcomb; from 1858 to 1859, the Rev. James Morton; in 1862, the Rev. Lewis Green; from 1865 to 1867, the Rev. F. B. Woodward; from 1872 to 1877, the Rev. Collis I. Potter; from 1883 to 1886, the Rev. William E. Johnson; from 1886 to 1888, the Rev. J. D. Gilliland; from 1888 to 1892, the Rev. William E. Hooker; from 1893 to 1895, the Rev. James Gammack, LL.D.; from 1896 to 1899, the Rev. George Henry Smith; from 1901 to 1907, the Rev. J. D. Gilliland.

HARWINTON

THIS parish was organized probably about 1787. For ten years it shared with St. Matthew's Church, East Plymouth, the labors of the Rev. Alexander V. Griswold, from 1795 till 1805. From that time for several years services were doubtless held here, and the presence of its lay delegates in the Convention of the diocese is noted in its Journal, but it does not give the names of

THE CLERGY OF LITCHFIELD COUNTY

the rectors. The Rev. G. C. V. Eastman was there in 1834; in 1843 and 1844, the Rev. William Zell; in 1846 and 1847, the Rev. H. V. Gardner; from 1851 to April, 1856, the Rev. Origen P. Holcomb; in 1857 and 1858, the Rev. James Morton; in 1862, the Rev. Lewis Green; in 1866, the Rev. H. C. Stowell; from 1868 to 1870, the Rev. Dr. Frederick Holcomb. For several years the Rev. J. Chauncey Linsley of Torrington has given the people a service occasionally during the summer.

KENT

ST ANDREW'S PARISH was organized February 22, 1808, but services of the Episcopal Church had been held there before that date and a church edifice had been erected. This is evident from the fact that the meeting to organize as a parish was warned to assemble at the Episcopal Church. The Rev. Sturges Gilbert was in charge from 1808 to 1816, the Rev. George B. Andrews from 1819 to 1832. The absence of full records for many years makes it impossible to give the names of the clergy who officiated in St. Andrew's from this time until 1854, when the Rev. H. S. Atwater became rector. He resigned in 1863. The Rev. X. Alanson Welton from 1866 to 1869; from 1871 to

THE EPISCOPAL CHURCH

1875, the Rev. Elisha Whittlesey; from 1876 to 1885, the Rev. Isaac C. Sturges; from 1885 to 1886, the Rev. Alban Richey; from 1886 to 1888, the Rev. George W. Griffith; from 1888 to 1895, the Rev. William F. Bielby; from 1895 to 1899, the Rev. Howard McDougal; from 1900, the present rector, the Rev. George Henry Smith.

LIME ROCK

THE parish of Trinity Church, Lime Rock, separated from St. John's Church, Salisbury, and organized as Trinity Church May 3, 1875. The first rector was the Rev. Millidge Walker, who assumed the charge of the parish February 27, 1876, remaining till 1884. From 1885 to 1895, the Rev. Richard F. Putnam; from 1895 to 1898, the Rev. Henry Tarrant; from 1900 to 1905, the Rev. Richmond H. Gesner; from 1905, the present rector, the Rev. George W. Griffith.

LITCHFIELD

THE introduction of the services of the Church of England into the town of Litchfield was due to Mr. John Davies, who came to this country from Kinton in

THE CLERGY OF LITCHFIELD COUNTY

Devonshire, England. He himself and his family were all strongly attached to the mother church. Mr. Davies, finding that a number of persons, offended by the disturbances caused by Mr. Whitefield's course, were well disposed toward the services of the English Church, gathered them together to consult with them in regard to introducing it into Litchfield. Dr. Johnson of Stratford, Dr. Cutler of West Haven, and Dr. Beach of Newtown, on invitation, came to Litchfield, held the Prayer-Book services, and administered the sacraments. Through the liberality of Mr. Davies especially, although assisted by others, a church was built in 1748. Probably the first clergyman who officiated in Litchfield with any regularity was the Rev. Solomon Palmer. He was a native of Branford and was graduated at Yale College in 1729. He was called to take charge of the Congregational Church in Cornwall in 1741. In addition to the salary voted to him, Mr. Palmer, as minister, was entitled to "a right of land"—about one fifty-third share of the town, probably about six hundred acres. Without doubt he derived from the cultivation of this land a large part of his maintenance—certainly a full supply of fuel; although then, as now, this could not be done without much hard labor. For over twelve years he ministered to this flock to their satisfaction, and it was a great surprise to them when, in 1754, Mr. Palmer gave up his ministry in Cornwall on the ground

THE EPISCOPAL CHURCH

that he had come to the conclusion that in order to give validity to his ministry he must receive episcopal ordination. Soon after this he went to England, and having been ordained by the Bishop of Bangor, he returned to this country. He was appointed missionary for this county by the Society for the Propagation of the Gospel in Foreign Parts. Mr. Palmer, supposing that the grant of land made to him in Cornwall when he became its first minister was his personal property, attempted on his return to exercise his right in it. This right, however, was disputed by the town of Cornwall, which claimed that he had forfeited his right by renouncing the Congregational ministry. A lawsuit was brought against him to recover the land, the claim being that he had broken a covenant made with the town. He was summoned "to appear before the county court to be held at Litchfield in and for the county of Litchfield on the fourth Tuesday of April next, then and there to answer . . . in a plea of a broken covenant." His answer was that by settling among the people as a teacher he, "by an act of the Assembly, became a proprietor, and the patent was and is absolute and unconditional." When Mr. Palmer expressed a willingness to relinquish some of his demands, a compromise was made. Among the papers of the Society for the Propagation of the Gospel are found letters which he later sent to its secretary, giving the amount of his expenses in the matter. These amounted to twenty-six pounds fourteen shillings and one penny. His letter also contains a request to the society to send to the mission at Litchfield "a Folio Bible and Common Prayer Book." Mr. Palmer gave most of his time to Litchfield, but in the year 1763 he went to New Haven to take charge of Trinity Church. He remained in New Haven for three years, and in 1766 came back to Litchfield, where he officiated until the time of his death in the year 1771—one of the three clergymen who have passed from their earthly ministry to the joys of Paradise while connected with this parish. During the three years which Mr. Palmer spent in New Haven, the Litchfield Mission was served by the Rev. Thomas Davies. He was a grandson of Mr. John Davies, through whose active interests services of the Church of England were first held in Litchfield. Thomas was born in Herefordshire, England, on the 21st of December, 1736, O. S. When his father, John Davies, Jr., came to this country, he lived in what is now a part of the town of Washington, near Romford Station. The neighborhood is still known as "Davies' Hollow," and some members of the family were buried in the cemetery a few rods from Romford Station. Thomas remained at home, getting such instruction as he could, until he entered Yale College in 1754. He pursued the usual college course and received

THE EPISCOPAL CHURCH

his degree as Bachelor of Arts September, 1758. He spent three years in a course of study as a candidate for orders. Of course he went to England for his ordination. He was made deacon on Sunday, August 23, 1761, by the Archbishop of Canterbury, and admitted to priest's orders the next day. In the abstract of the proceedings of the Propagation Society for the year 1761, mention is made of the "Rev. Mr. Davies, Itinerant Missionary in Litchfield County and parts adjacent." He is spoken of as "a hopeful young man, strongly recommended by Dr. Johnson, Mr. Palmer and others as truly worthy of the society's notice and encouragement." He received his appointment from the society in the following words: "Agreed the 18th September, 1761, that Mr. Davies be appointed Missionary to the Churches of New Milford, Roxbury, Sharon, New Preston and New Fairfield in Litchfield County, Connecticut." In this commission the mission at Litchfield is not mentioned, but that it was very soon after included by formal appointment or by Mr. Davies's zeal appears from the fact that a letter sent to him by the Secretary of the Society for the Propagation of the Gospel informs him that two quarto Bibles and two folio Common Prayer Books had been sent to him, one for the church in Sharon, and the other for the church in Litchfield. Mr. Davies took up his residence in New Milford. He probably never lived in Litchfield, though he was the missionary in charge, and it was where he most earnestly and successfully labored. This is evident from the fact that in 1763 he reported that there were sixty-one families under his care and in these families were fifty-seven communicants. His private diary also records the names of many persons baptized there during his ministry. Two or three times this diary records his officiating on "St. Pompion's Day," by which title he facetiously named the annual Thanksgiving Day, for a reason of which all dwellers in Litchfield County will recognize the appropriateness. Mr. Davies's earthly ministry was all too short. His frequent journeys, mostly on horseback, through winter storms and summer heat, executing the duties of his office whenever opportunity offered, told too fatally on a constitution not over-strong. On the 12th of May, 1766, in less than six years after his ordination, in the thirtieth year of his life, he passed from earth and was buried in New Milford. A monument erected to his memory in the New Milford cemetery bears an inscription ending thus: "Vita bene acta jucundissima est recordatio." It was the opinion of the Rev. Truman Marsh, who later was rector at New Milford and also at Litchfield, that Mr. Davies's ability as a preacher and organizer, with his affable and winning manners, would have secured for him, had he lived, the honor of being the first American bishop.

THE EPISCOPAL CHURCH

After the death of Mr. Davies, the Rev. Solomon Palmer returned to Litchfield, where he preached until the time of his death in 1771. At the outbreak of the Revolutionary War the mission at Litchfield was in charge of the Rev. James Nichols, a native of Waterbury. He was graduated from Yale College in 1771. He was the last man who went from Connecticut to England to secure ordination. It is not known that he resided in Litchfield during the war, probably not, for the church records show that for the greater part of that time services were rendered by lay readers. However, after peace was declared, Mr. Nichols was in Litchfield and renewed the services of the church. A little later he presented an address to the General Assembly asking for the appointment of a prominent churchman, Mr. Daniel Landon, as justice of the peace, "wishing," as the petition reads, "the favor of a justice of the peace to adorn the Society."

After peace was declared the connection of the mission at Litchfield with the society in England, which had so long contributed to its support, came to an end. On the 26th of October, 1784, "The First Episcopal Society of Litchfield" was organized and secured the services as lay reader of Mr. Ashbel Baldwin, a candidate for holy orders. Mr. Baldwin was graduated from Yale College in 1776, and for a part of the time during the war was stationed at Litchfield as a quarter-

THE CLERGY OF LITCHFIELD COUNTY

master in charge of army supplies. He was made deacon at the first ordination held by Bishop Seabury after his return from Scotland, where he had been consecrated bishop. This ordination was held at Middletown, August 3, 1785. Mr. Baldwin remained in Litchfield until 1793. He was Secretary of the Convention of the Diocese of Connecticut for thirty years, and of the House of Clerical and Lay Deputies of the General Convention for twelve years. He died in 1846, in his eighty-ninth year.

This parish had an uneventful history during the nineteenth century. About the beginning of it the work in the three villages of Litchfield, Bantam, and Milton, which up to this time had been in the charge of one man, was divided. St. Michael's, at the center, demanded the time and energy of one man, and the work at Bantam and Milton required the services of another. But the three parishes are still one ecclesiastical society, and they have an equal share in the income of invested funds. In St. Michael's, Litchfield, the succession has been as follows: the Rev. Mr. Baldwin, in charge from 1785 to 1793; the Rev. Dr. David Butler, 1794 to 1799; the Rev. Truman Marsh, from 1799 to 1829; the Rev. Isaac Jones (associate rector), from 1812 to 1826; the Rev. Dr. John S. Stone (associate rector), from 1826 to 1829; the Rev. William Lucas, 1829 to 1832; the Rev. Dr. Samuel Fuller, from 1832 to 1837

Congregational Church, Litchfield

THE EPISCOPAL CHURCH

and from 1845 to 1849; the Rev. Dr. William Payne, from 1838 to 1845; the Rev. Dr. Benjamin W. Stone, from 1849 to 1851; the Rev. Dr. John J. Brandagee, from 1851 to 1854; the Rev. Junius M. Willey, from 1855 to 1858; the Rev. H. N. Hudson, from 1858 to 1860; the Rev. William S. Southgate, from 1860 to 1864; the Rev. William Stevens Perry, from 1864 to 1869 (afterward Bishop of Iowa); the Rev. Dr. C. S. Henry, from 1870 to 1873; the Rev. G. M. Wilkins, from 1874 to 1879; the Rev. Dr. S. O. Seymour, from 1879 to 1881; the Rev. Dr. L. P. Bissell, from 1882 to 1893. In 1893 Dr. Seymour again took charge and is still the rector.

The following clergymen have held the two parishes of Bantam and Milton as one charge: the Rev. David G. Tomlinson, from 1831 to 1835; the Rev. Amos Beach, from 1836 to 1837; the Rev. Hilliard Bryant, from 1837 to 1840; the Rev. Emery M. Porter, from September, 1842, to 1843; the Rev. Frederick D. Harriman, from 1848 to 1850; the Rev. George W. Nichols, from 1850 to 1851; the Rev. Asa Griswold, from January, 1852, to November, 1852; the Rev. Daniel E. Brown, from 1853 to 1857; the Rev. John R. Williams, from 1858 to 1860; the Rev. J. A. Wainwright, from 1860 to 1861; the Rev. Dr. J. D. Berry, from 1864 to 1866; the Rev. William L. Peck, from 1866 to 1871; the Rev. Hiram Stone, from 1873 to 1903; the Rev.

THE CLERGY OF LITCHFIELD COUNTY

J. H. Jackson, from 1904 to 1905; the Rev. John O. Ferris, from 1905 to 1908; the Rev. Clarence H. Beers, the present rector, from March 29, 1908.

MARBLEDALE

THIS parish was organized in 1784. It was called at that time and until 1857 New Preston. The first notice which our printed journals give is in 1793, where it is recorded that the parish of New Preston had not adopted in full the Constitution of the Diocese of Connecticut. Evidently they soon acceded to the remainder, for their delegates were present at the Convention held in 1797, and later in 1801, 1802, 1803, and in 1807, when it reported as its grand levy $8300, there being at that time only six other parishes in the diocese reporting a larger "grand list." In 1809 and 1810 the Rev. Benjamin Benham had charge of the parish; from 1813 to 1816, the Rev. Sturges Gilbert; from 1820 to 1826, the Rev. George B. Andrews; in 1827, the Rev. Ezra Kellogg; in 1829, the Rev. Harry Finch; in 1832, the Rev. H. S. Atwater; in 1836 and 1837, the Rev. Enoch Huntington, rector of St. John's, New Milford; from August, 1839, to 1843, the Rev. George S. Gordon; from August, 1846, to 1848, the Rev. William

THE EPISCOPAL CHURCH

Long; from 1849 to June, 1853, the Rev. James L. Scott, and, after an interval of a year, from July, 1854, to 1867; from August, 1868, to November, 1869, the Rev. Henry C. Randall; from Easter, 1870, to September, 1872, the Rev. Charles Husband; in 1873, the Rev. J. N. Marvin; from 1875 to 1882, the Rev. William L. Peck; from 1883 to 1885, the Rev. Robert L. Mathison; in 1889, the Rev. J. D. Gilliland; from 1890 to 1893, the Rev. George A. Alcott; in 1894, the Rev. Reuben B. Whipple; in 1895, the Rev. Edward T. Mathison; from July, 1896, to 1906, the Rev. Thomas S. Ockford; from December, 1906, the present rector, the Rev. William E. Hooker.

NEW MILFORD

THE REV. STANLEY GRISWOLD, pastor of the Congregational Church in New Milford, states in his "Century Sermon" that there were churchmen in the town from its settlement in 1707. There is, however, no record of any separate congregation or regular services for many years. After the Rev. John Beach had established the services of the Church of England in Newtown, fifteen miles distant, in 1732, many of the church families in New Milford used to journey to Newtown on Saturdays to attend Sunday services. To accommodate these fami-

THE CLERGY OF LITCHFIELD COUNTY

lies the Rev. Mr. Beach began services in New Milford in 1742, sending Mr. Barzilla Dean as a lay reader. The services were held in a private house.

The first church edifice was built in 1744, and the congregation remained under the care of the Rev. Mr. Beach until 1754, when a resident minister was secured, the Rev. Solomon Palmer. After five years Mr. Palmer removed to Litchfield and was succeeded in 1762 by the Rev. Thomas Davies. The ministry of Mr. Davies was a brief one, the span of his life being but thirty years. In four years of his ministry in New Milford, however, he seems to have accomplished much, for the congregation outgrew the church building, and work was begun upon a new and larger one. Mr. Davies was succeeded by the Rev. Richard (or Richard Samuel) Clarke, who remained in charge for twenty years. The new church building was so far completed that services were held in it; but the stormy days preceding the Revolutionary War and of the war itself were not propitious for the Church of England in the colony, and the church building was not finally completed until 1793. Mr. Clarke was a Tory in political conviction, and after struggling against many discouragements resigned in 1787 and went to Nova Scotia. For a time the church was closed.

In 1790 regular services were again maintained under the rectorship of the Rev. Truman Marsh. The ten

THE EPISCOPAL CHURCH

years of his ministry were years of quiet growth and strengthening. The church was completed and consecrated by Bishop Seabury in 1793.

In 1799, to the great regret of his congregation, Mr. Marsh relinquished his labors in New Milford and removed to Litchfield.

The parish was now to experience a test even more severe than that of the days of the Revolution. The colonies, having become independent of Great Britain, could no longer look to the great English missionary society of the English Church, as they had done, to find and help maintain their clergy, and so few were the clergy at this time that in spite of great effort the parish could not secure a minister for many years. The fact that it survived shows how great was its latent strength. At last, on Easter Day, March 29, 1807, Mr. Benjamin Benham, a candidate for holy orders, was secured. Mr. Benham was ordained priest in August, 1808, and continued in charge of the parish for nearly twenty years.

Mr. Benham was followed by the Rev. Enoch Huntington, who bears the honorable record of having been rector of St. John's Parish longer than any other clergyman. During his rectorship, which lasted until 1848, a new church was built in 1837, which still stands, though used now for commercial purposes. To Mr. Huntington's long and devoted services the parish of to-day owes much of its strength.

THE CLERGY OF LITCHFIELD COUNTY

For a few years at this period of its history the parish experienced frequent changes of rectors.

The Rev. Cyrus Munson took charge in June, 1848, and died the following August. He was buried on the day that had been set for his wedding-day.

The Rev. W. H. Rees began his work here January 11, 1849, and resigned April 2, 1850, to accept work in Branford, Connecticut.

The Rev. G. B. Hayden supplied the parish for a year, but declined to take permanent charge.

The Rev. D. P. Sanford began his rectorship in August, 1851, and resigned in 1853 to accept a parish in Brooklyn, New York.

The Rev. John W. Hoffman became rector February 1, 1854, and resigned at Easter, 1856.

After this trying period of eight years, in which five different men had ministered to the parish, there succeeded another long period of rest and growth under the faithful ministry of the Rev. C. G. Acly, whose rectorship dated from August, 1856, to March, 1876. During this time many improvements were made and the number of communicants greatly increased.

After the resignation of Mr. Acly, the parish was not long in securing another minister, for on May 1, 1876, the Rev. A. S. Clark took charge and remained as rector until October 27, 1879.

In less than a month after the resignation of Mr.

THE EPISCOPAL CHURCH

Clark, another rector was called, the Rev. Edward L. Wells, D.D. By him was started the project of building a new stone church. Plans were drawn and accepted, but before work was begun Dr. Wells died in 1880, having been rector less than one year.

The Rev. Edward R. Brown succeeded him and entered with great vigor upon the work of building a new church. Owing largely to his enthusiasm and determination, a beautiful granite church was built on Gothic lines, seating over five hundred people. It was completed and paid for by the congregation within two years, and was consecrated March 15, 1883. In 1890, after nine years of indefatigable parish work, Mr. Brown's health broke down, and he resigned the rectorship.

The Rev. E. P. Sanford succeeded Mr. Brown, and took charge of the parish in 1891. He was greatly beloved by his congregation, who mourned his early death in 1895.

The present rector is the Rev. John F. Plumb, who took charge April 28, 1895.

In thus tracing the history of the parish from the early days to the present, giving little more than names and dates of rectorships, one feels that one would like to write a real history of the parish and speak of the devoted lives of laymen and women, who constituted the true life and strength of the parish through all

THE CLERGY OF LITCHFIELD COUNTY

vicissitudes, but that would constitute a volume in itself, and must be omitted here. With more than a century and a half of vigorous life behind it, the parish to-day stands ready to meet the problems of the present and the future, confident that God, who has led it hitherto, will lead it ever forward to greater usefulness in making known to men his righteousness and his kingdom.

IN November, 1885, a congregation under the name of All Saints was organized, a stone church having been built, largely as a memorial of Judge David C. Sanford. In December, 1885, the Rev. John A. Crockett became minister in charge, and remained until October, 1888. At Easter, 1889, the Rev. Frank B. Draper took the charge. In 1891 the congregation of All Saints became an organized parish in union with the Diocese of Connecticut, the Rev. Frank B. Draper rector, which position he held until June 2, 1901. From 1901 to 1906, the Rev. Cranston Brenton; from 1906 to 1907, the Rev. Marmaduke Hare, M.D.; for a few months in 1908, the Rev. Jacob A. Biddle, when the Rev. Frank B. Draper, the present rector, was again elected.

NORTHFIELD

THIS parish was organized as early as 1793; still, little of its early history is on record. At different times,

THE EPISCOPAL CHURCH

namely, in 1816, 1817, 1824, 1825, 1831, and 1832, the Rev. Frederick Holcomb officiated here; in 1834, the Rev. James Keeler. In 1835-36 the Rev. William Watson was in charge; from 1837 to 1839, the Rev. T. W. Snow; from 1839 to 1844, the Rev. Isaac H. Tuttle; from 1844 to 1846, the Rev. Frederick Holcomb; in 1847-48, the Rev. Dr. J. D. Berry; in 1848-49, the Rev. George W. Nichols; from April, 1851, to January, 1852, the Rev. Asa Griswold; from 1853 to Easter, 1861, the Rev. Frederick Holcomb; from 1862 to 1863, the Rev. Lewis Green; from 1864 to 1867, the Rev. H. C. Stowell; from Easter, 1868, to Easter, 1869, the Rev. C. C. Adams; from 1872 to 1876, the Rev. William L. Bostwick. From 1880 to 1883 the Rev. S. O. Seymour, rector at Litchfield, had the oversight of the parish, a lay reader having the Sunday services. From 1885 to 1889, the Rev. D. L. Sanford; in 1890-91, the Rev. William E. Hooker. From 1892 to 1900 the Rev. A. T. Parsons of Thomaston was in charge; from 1900 to 1901, the Rev. George Buck; from Easter, 1902, the present rector, the Rev. Adelbert P. Chapman.

PINE MEADOW

ST. JOHN'S PARISH, Pine Meadow, in the town of New Hartford, was organized November 20, 1850. The

THE CLERGY OF LITCHFIELD COUNTY

first church edifice was burned December 23, 1859. A new church was built, and the first service was held in it on Christmas Eve, 1861. The rectors have been: from Easter, 1851, to July, 1857, the Rev. John H. Betts; from April, 1858, to May, 1860, the Rev. Enoch Huntington; from November, 1861, to October, 1862, the Rev. Myron A. Johnson; from November, 1862, to March, 1863, the Rev. I. S. Judd; from May, 1863, to April, 1865, the Rev. DeLancy G. Rice; from 1866 to 1868, the Rev. Jesse C. Heald; from April, 1869, to May, 1880, the Rev. John H. Betts; from 1880 to 1882, the Rev. Thomas A. Porter; from 1882 to 1887, the Rev. C. W. Colton; from 1887 to 1890, the Rev. T. D. Martin, Jr.; from 1890 to 1893, the Rev. R. B. Whipple; from 1895 to 1898, the Rev. Herbert M. Smith; from 1899 to 1904, the Rev. Henry Tarrant; from 1904, the Rev. Henry M. Stanley, the present rector.

PLYMOUTH

It was in 1740 that the services of the Church of England were first brought into this town. Three years before, in 1737, nineteen petitioners living in Plymouth, who were accustomed to attend the Congregational Church in Waterbury, desired for themselves the privi-

St. Michael's, Litchfield

THE EPISCOPAL CHURCH

lege of holding services during three winter months in their own town. So, in 1739, they were incorporated into a parish by the name of Northbury. They formed an ecclesiastical society and erected a building in which services were held on Sunday, while on week-days, in a room on the second story, a school was kept. The minister, the Rev. Samuel Todd, was not altogether acceptable, and finally eleven out of the nineteen proprietors of the building declared for the Church of England. They also took possession of the building, and by a vote excluded the services of Mr. Todd. The ejected proprietors received a promise of aid in building another house, and when they did so this promise is said to have been redeemed in a manner entirely satisfactory to them.

The first church edifice was built in "The Hollow," as Thomaston was then called. The mission before the Revolution was served by the Rev. Messrs. Theophilus Morris, James Lyon, Richard Mansfield, James Scovell, and James Nichols. All of these were missionaries under appointment from the English Society for Propagating the Gospel. After the Revolutionary War was ended fifty-seven men organized a parish and called it St. Peter's. In 1796–97 a new church, the present one, was built. The following clergymen served the parish in this order, though exact dates cannot be given, namely, Nathan B. Burgess, Roger Searle (who afterward went as a home missionary to Ohio), and Rodney Rossiter.

THE CLERGY OF LITCHFIELD COUNTY

Following these, the Rev. Robert W. Harris, the Rev. Joseph T. Clark, the Rev. Gurdon S. Coit, the Rev. Norman Pinney, and the Rev. Allen C. Morgan officiated a few months each. From 1831 to 1837 the Rev. Dr. D. Burham was rector; from 1837 to 1851, the Rev. William Watson; from 1851 to 1854, the Rev. S. D. Denison; from 1854 to 1855, the Rev. A. B. Goodrich; from 1856 to 1858, the Rev. S. K. Miller; from 1859 to 1861, the Rev. Dr. J. D. Berry; from 1862 to 1863, the Rev. David F. Lumsden; from 1864 to 1868, the Rev. Benjamin Eastwood; from 1869 to 1873, the Rev. Porter Thomas; from 1873 to 1874, the Rev. Lester M. Dorman; from 1874 to 1876, the Rev. S. Brainerd Duffield; from 1876 to 1878, the Rev. John M. Bates; from October, 1878, to October, 1888, the Rev. J. D. Gilliland; from October, 1888, to October, 1892, the Rev. William E. Hooker; from November, 1892, to October, 1895, the Rev. A. T. Gammack, LL.D.; from November, 1895, to March, 1900, the Rev. George Henry Smith; from July, 1900, to June, 1908, the Rev. J. D. Gilliland; from September, 1908, the present rector, the Rev. Herbert L. Mitchell.

RIVERTON

SERVICES were held in Riverton, then called Hitchcocksville, about 1830. Delegates were present from this

THE EPISCOPAL CHURCH

village at the Diocesan Convention of 1830, who reported that a church building was nearly ready for use. The parish has never been a strong one. The Rev. Isaac Jones, rector in 1837, reported in 1838 forty-six families connected with the parish, but adds, "This vicinity is in all respects missionary ground." From 1839 to 1840 the Rev. Silas Blaisdale was rector. From June, 1842, to Easter, 1843, the Rev. Henry Zell reports that he had temporary charge. From 1843 to 1846 the Rev. W. H. Frisbie had charge; from 1847 to 1849, the Rev. Jonathan Coe, 2d. From 1878 to 1879 the Rev. Carlos S. Linsley resided in Riverton. Since that time the rectors of Pine Meadow have given more or less of their time to this mission.

ROXBURY

THE Episcopal Church in Roxbury had its beginning as early as 1740, the Rev. Mr. Beach of Newtown holding the first services there. The first church edifice was built in 1763, near by the old cemetery. The Rev. Thomas Davies gave some part of his time to the care of this parish. Later a new church building was erected in the center of Roxbury, which, with improvements made in 1861, still stands. Who succeeded Mr. Davies in his labors cannot be told. The following names and dates,

THE CLERGY OF LITCHFIELD COUNTY

with many intervals, tell the story: In 1794 Roswell Ransom was present at the Convention of the Connecticut Clergy and Laymen as a lay delegate. Amos Squires is reported as present in 1798. No clerical names appear in the Journal until 1816, when the Rev. Joseph D. Welton was in charge for about a year. Then for ten years, from 1817 to 1827, the Rev. Sturges Gilbert was rector; for one year, 1825, the Rev. Edward C. Bull officiated. In 1829-30 the Rev. William Lucas held the rectorship; from 1841 to 1847, the Rev. George L. Foote; from Easter, 1851, to 1852, the Rev. H. T. M. Whitesides; from 1852 to 1853, the Rev. Abel Nichols; from November, 1854, to 1856, the Rev. Merritt H. Wellman; from 1859 to 1860, the Rev. W. H. Cook; from Easter, 1860, to June, 1870, the Rev. Collis I. Potter; from 1873 to 1874, the Rev. Sheldon Davis; from 1875 to 1892, the Rev. William C. Cooley; from 1892, the present rector, the Rev. Walter Downs Humphrey.

SALISBURY

IT is probable that services of the Episcopal Church were held in Salisbury before the middle of the eighteenth century, but it was not until the coming of the Rev. Thomas Davies, who seems to have taken the

THE EPISCOPAL CHURCH

whole county as his parish, that services were held here regularly. For a time, at least, Mr. Davies officiated here as often as once a month, but after his death only occasional services were held till long after the Revolutionary War. In 1809 the Rev. Sturges Gilbert was assigned to the care of the parish in connection with Sharon and Kent. In 1822 the Rev. George B. Andrews was in charge, and during his rectorship a new brick church was built. He was followed by the Rev. Stephen Beach in 1824, who remained rector until 1833. From 1833 to May, 1837, the Rev. Lucius M. Purdy was in charge. Beginning with 1837, four clergymen, namely, the Rev. Charles W. Bradley, the Rev. S. T. Carpenter, the Rev. David N. Devins, and the Rev. William Warland, followed in quick succession. From April, 1846, to Easter, 1854, the Rev. George H. Nichols was in charge; from 1854 to 1858, the Rev. Ruel H. Tuttle; from 1858 to 1862, the Rev. Dr. Samuel F. Jarvis; from March 29, 1863, to September, 1871, the Rev. Jonathan A. Wainwright; from 1871 to 1882, the Rev. William Allen Johnson; from February 1, 1883, to 1902, the Rev. James H. George; from 1902 to 1903, the Rev. Henry S. Habersham; from November 8, 1903, to 1908, the Rev. Henry H. Davies; from 1908, the present rector, the Rev. David N. Kirkby.

THE CLERGY OF LITCHFIELD COUNTY

SHARON

ON the 14th of April, 1755, the town of Sharon gave to the Episcopalians leave to erect a church at the head of the street, near to Captain King's. This building stood for nearly forty years. Services were held in it by the Rev. Ebenezer Dibble, the Rev. Solomon Palmer, and the Rev. Thomas Davies, missionaries of the Propagation Society. During the Revolutionary War the building was deserted and never again used for public worship. At a meeting duly warned and held at the Academy, May 18, 1809, a parish was organized. The Rev. Sturges Gilbert held service in the Academy every other Sunday. In 1812 steps were taken to build a church, and early in 1814 it was so far finished that service was held in it. It was not finished on the inside nor furnished until 1819. The following clergymen have served as rectors: in 1818, the Rev. George B. Andrews; in 1833, the Rev. Lucius M. Purdy; in 1837, the Rev. Charles W. Bradley; in 1839, the Rev. S. T. Carpenter; in 1844, the Rev. Martin Moody; in 1849, the Rev. Alonzo G. Shears; in 1852, the Rev. Ezra Jones; in 1856, the Rev. Louis French; in 1858, the Rev. John V. Stryker; from 1866 to May, 1869, the Rev. Henry R. Howard; from September, 1869, to 1871, the Rev. Dr. David MacDonald; from 1871

THE EPISCOPAL CHURCH

to 1873, the Rev. Joseph W. Hyde; from 1873 to 1876, the Rev. Edwin J. K. Lessell; from 1877 to 1882, the Rev. Percival H. Whaley; from 1882 to 1883, the Rev. Charles Ferris; from 1885 to 1893, the Rev. George Rumney; from 1894 to 1900, the Rev. George C. Griswold; from 1901 to June, 1905, the Rev. H. W. Hutcheson; from 1905 to November, 1907, the Rev. James Buchanan Nies, Ph.D.; from 1907 to September, 1908, the Rev. Lawrence H. Schwab. The Rev. Dr. D. P. Morgan is now in charge of the parish.

THOMASTON

SERVICES of the Episcopal Church were first regularly held in Thomaston by the Rev. Benjamin Eastwood in 1866. In the next year the building formerly occupied by the Methodists was bought, and a parish organized January 2, 1869. The Rev. David Bishop was rector from 1869 to February 1, 1874; the Rev. Thomas Ockford from February 10, 1874, to 1883; the Rev. David L. Sanford from 1883 to 1890. The Rev. Arthur T. Parsons, the present rector, assumed charge in the winter of 1890.

TORRINGTON

THE parish of Trinity Church was organized February 21, 1843, worshiping at first in the Brick Academy. In

THE CLERGY OF LITCHFIELD COUNTY

the next year a church was built on the corner of Water and Prospect streets. The first rector, the Rev. Henry Zell, was elected January 6, 1845, and remained until Easter, 1848. The Rev. David P. Sanford was rector from April 8, 1849, to 1850; the Rev. J. S. Covell from August, 1851, to October, 1855. The parish was vacant until October, 1858, when the Rev. Mr. Covell was recalled and remained till 1863. In April, 1864, the Rev. Mr. Sanford was recalled, who remained until September 13, 1868. Soon after, the Rev. Benjamin Eastwood was elected, and continued in charge until 1874. In June, 1874, the Rev. Henry B. Ensworth became rector, but remained only until December, 1874. September 1, 1876, the Rev. Henry M. Sherman became rector, and remained in charge until 1890. From 1891 to 1895 the Rev. Melville K. Bailey was rector. On the 1st of July, 1895, the present rector, the Rev. J. Chauncey Linsley, took charge. During his rectorship the new stone church and the parish house have been erected.

WASHINGTON

THE REV. THOMAS DAVIES held services in Washington as early as 1762. His father, Mr. John Davies, deeded land in the neighborhood of Davies Hollow, on which a church was built about three years before his

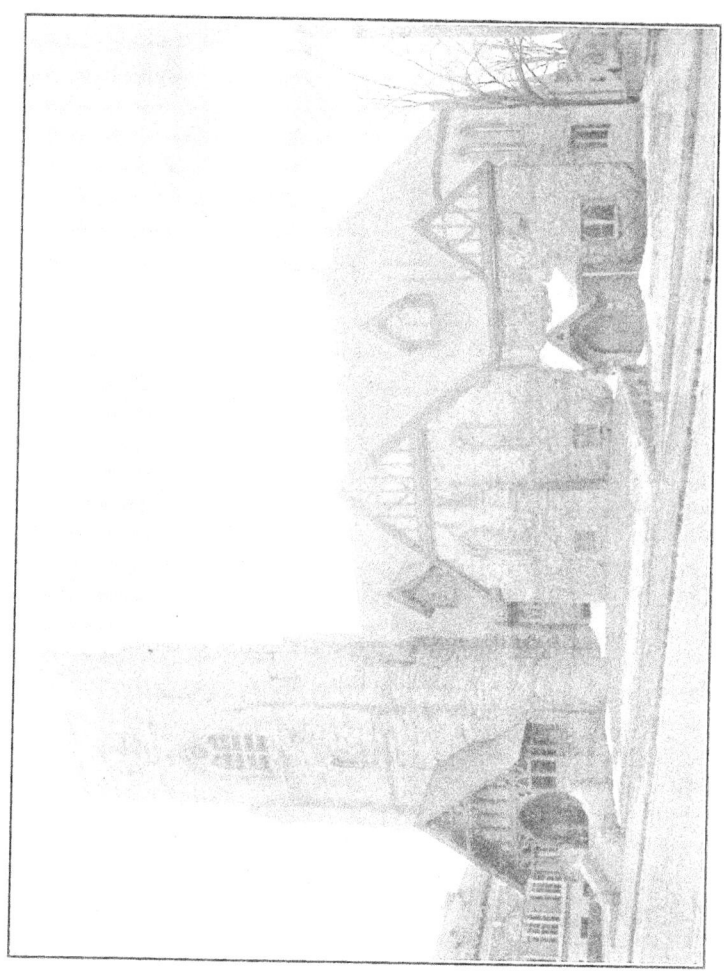

Trinity, Torrington

THE EPISCOPAL CHURCH

death in 1758. In 1813 this church was moved to Washington Green, where it still stands. At this time it was named St. John's Church. No complete list of the clergy who have had charge of it can be given, for the early records were lost. Beginning with the year 1840, the Rev. George S. Gordon was in charge for one year. From 1842 to 1846 the Rev. George L. Foote held services once each month; from 1847 to 1848, the Rev. William Long; from 1849 to 1853, the Rev. James L. Scott. The parish was vacant in 1854, but Mr. Scott was again in charge from 1855 to 1867. In 1868, 1869, and 1870 the parish was vacant. In 1871 the Rev. John D. Gilliland was in charge; in 1872, the Rev. A. L. Rice (Royce); from 1875 to 1882, the Rev. William L. Peck; from 1884 to 1888, the Rev. Charles Doupé; from 1888 to 1896, the Rev. William G. Spencer; from May, 1896, to Easter, 1899, the Rev. E. A. Angell; from 1899 to 1905, the Rev. Percy G. H. Robinson; from October 1, 1905, the present rector, the Rev. Theodore M. Peck, a son of a former rector, the Rev. William L. Peck.

WATERTOWN

IN 1764 the first steps were taken which resulted in establishing the services of the Episcopal Church in Watertown. (Dr. Beardsley's History, p. 238.) The

THE CLERGY OF LITCHFIELD COUNTY

next year the first church building was erected. Twenty-nine years later, in 1794, another took its place, which was consecrated by Bishop Seabury November 18. This was used until October 28, 1855, when the congregation entered upon the use of the third building, which is still standing. From 1759 to 1785 the Rev. James Scovill was in charge. He was followed by the Rev. Chauncey Prindle, who remained until 1804. The Rev. Russell Wheeler was rector from 1805 to 1814; the Rev. Frederick Holcomb, D.D., from 1814 to 1839; the Rev. Dr. N. S. Richardson from 1839 to 1845; Dr. Holcomb again from 1845 to 1849; the Rev. Horace H. Reid from 1850 to 1856; the Rev. Dr. Benjamin W. Stone from 1856 to 1859; the Rev. Dr. H. Lewis, from 1860 to 1874, having as his assistant the Rev. William L. Peck from 1871 to 1874; the Rev. Dr. S. D. McConnell from 1874 to 1876; the Rev. James Stoddard from 1876 to 1886. The present rector, the Rev. H. N. Cunningham, came in 1886, with an interval of four years, 1890 to 1894, which was occupied by the Rev. John L. Nichols.

WINSTED

CHURCH services were held in Winsted in the year 1847, but it was not until 1848 that a parish was organized and a church built. In 1849 the Rev. Jona-

THE EPISCOPAL CHURCH

than Coe, 2d, was in charge and remained until 1852. In 1854 the Rev. James Wells Coe was rector; from 1855 to 1859, the Rev. James R. Coe; in 1860, the Rev. Dr. D. H. Short; in 1865, the Rev. John H. Anketell; from 1866 to 1867, the Rev. William H. Williams; from 1868 to May, 1870, the Rev. William H. Lewis, Jr.; from July, 1870, to 1873, the Rev. David P. Sanford; from 1875 to 1878, the Rev. Frederick S. Jewell, Ph.D.; from 1879 to 1880, the Rev. F. W. Harriman; from 1881 to 1901, the Rev. G. M. Stanley; from 1902, the present rector, the Rev. Seth Wolcott Linsley.

WOODBURY

AT an early date, some time before the year 1740, there were in Woodbury a few people attached to the Church of England. The clergyman who ministered to them occasionally was the Rev. Dr. John Beach of Newtown. The first church edifice was erected on the hill between Roxbury and a district called Transylvania, but when in 1747 the Congregationalists built a new church, the old First Church was used by the Episcopalians for public worship until the erection of the present church in 1785. In 1771 the Rev. John Rutgers Marshall, a native of New York and a graduate of King's College, returned from England, whither he had gone to secure

THE CLERGY OF LITCHFIELD COUNTY

holy orders. He was appointed by the Society for the Propagation of the Gospel in Foreign Parts missionary to Woodbury, and for eighteen years so wisely administered the affairs of the parish that it has always been a strong and vigorous one, retaining and illustrating the principles upon which it was founded. In connection with this parish, it is well to anticipate a little, for here occurred an event which the Episcopal Church in this country considers the most momentous in its history: As soon as the Revolutionary War was ended, the Church of England felt that her connection with the church in this country had come to an end, especially in the matter of supplying funds for the support of the clergymen to whom she had given her orders. The missionary society, which had so liberally contributed to the welfare of the church, was by its charter limited to the support of colonies of the kingdom of Great Britain. Consequently the recognition of the independence of those colonies closed this source of supply. At the end of the war there were thirteen clergymen still in charge of parishes in Connecticut. When peace was declared, the question of securing a bishop for the church became a pressing one. At the suggestion of the Rev. Mr. Marshall, or because Woodbury was a quiet place in which important business might be transacted without attracting public notice, ten of the clergy of Connecticut met there on the 25th of March, 1783,

THE EPISCOPAL CHURCH

to consult about securing a bishop for Connecticut. As the result of this council, one of the number, the Rev. Mr. Jarvis of Middletown, was sent to New York on this business. First, he tried to prevail upon the Rev. Dr. Leaming of New York to undertake this duty, and when he, for good reasons, declined, Mr. Jarvis, according to instructions given, prevailed upon the Rev. Samuel Seabury to go to England to secure, if possible, consecration as Bishop of the Episcopal Church in Connecticut. The English bishops, for political reasons, felt unable to comply with the urgent request which Dr. Seabury presented from the Connecticut clergy. So, after a year of unavailing effort, he went to Scotland, and there, in Aberdeen, November 14, 1784, Dr. Seabury was consecrated by three Scottish bishops, the Scottish Church being independent of the English Government. The house in Woodbury in which the ten clergymen met and chose Dr. Seabury is still standing as a memorial of this event, the property of the Diocese of Connecticut.

The Rev. John Marshall died on January 21, 1789. Soon after this the Rev. Mr. Sayre influenced the people of St. Paul's Church to object to adopting the Constitution under which, at New Haven, in June, 1792, the bishop, clergy, and laity organized as the Diocese of Connecticut. Believing in the sincerity of Mr. Sayre's course, they refused to accept this Constitution; but

THE CLERGY OF LITCHFIELD COUNTY

afterward better counsels prevailed, and having counseled with a committee appointed by the Convention, the parish with unanimity acceded to it and came into union with the Convention. The names of those who served this parish at the beginning of the nineteenth century are not known to the writer. In 1810 the Rev. Joseph D. Welton was ordained and took charge of the parish until 1817. He was succeeded by the Rev. Sturges Gilbert in 1817, who remained in charge until 1827; the Rev. William Lucas from 1828 to 1830. In 1830 the Rev. Ulysses M. Wheeler officiated for a few months; from 1834 to 1835, the Rev. J. Dowdney; from 1839 to May, 1845, the Rev. Solomon G. Hitchcock; from October, 1845, to 1846, the Rev. Richard Cox; from 1846 to 1847, the Rev. David P. Sanford; from 1847 to Easter, 1848, the Rev. Charles Putnam; from 1848 to 1849, the Rev. Pierre T. Babbitt; from October, 1849, to February, 1853, the Rev. Robert C. Rogers; from 1853 to 1855, the Rev. Frederick D. Harriman; from 1855 to 1859, the Rev. Curtis T. Woodruff; from March, 1860, to 1862, the Rev. George Rumney; from Easter, 1863, to Easter, 1872, the Rev. John Purvis; from 1874 to 1877, the Rev. J. G. Jacocks; from 1878 to 1879, the Rev. E. T. Sanford; from 1880 to 1883, the Rev. J. Francis George; from 1883 to 1886, the Rev. Dr. R. Nelson; from 1887 to 1889, the Rev. W. H. Dean; from 1890 to July,

Episcopal Church, Plymouth

THE EPISCOPAL CHURCH

1895, the Rev. J. Chauncey Linsley; from 1896 to 1898, the Rev. J. T. Hargraves; from April, 1898, to 1905, the Rev. Leander R. Sheffield; from 1906 to 1908, the Rev. J. H. Barnard. The parish is now vacant.

CHAPTER XI

BAPTISTS

HE ways of schism were not easy in the early history of Litchfield County. The poverty and hardships of the pioneers made it sufficiently difficult to support the parish church in each community, without dividing their resources. There were in the eighteenth century only two competing sects, Episcopal and Baptist. The Church of England ministers were missionaries, sustained by an English society, and when they gained an entrance could hold their position by a systematic and organized plan.

The Baptists, without organization or money, had to make up by zeal and sacrifice for the lack of other advantages. Their ministers were usually young men without education, who could travel from parish

BAPTISTS

to parish appealing to disaffected or unorganized people in the districts more remote from the regular meeting-places. I am able to find but little record of these men, though indications of their influence remain in many towns, where traditional sites of Baptist churches are found, or old graveyards bear witness to the former lives of ministers and members. The Baptist Church in Litchfield at Bantam Falls is the successor of two earlier Baptist churches, one in Northfield and the other in Morris. These churches of course had ministers, but I know not their names. The present church was organized in 1852, and is usually associated with similar churches in East Cornwall and Cornwall Hollow. An early Baptist church in Barkhamsted was afterward merged in the one at New Hartford. Baptist churches in Bridgewater and Roxbury became long ago extinct.

In the town of New Milford three Baptist churches were organized in the first half of the nineteenth century, at Northville, Merryall, and Gaylordsville. I think two of them are still existent. The early Baptist ministers were, as I have said, mainly young men with zeal and without education. Their names do not mean much to history, but they achieved some results of considerable importance, mainly perhaps as a counter-irritant in developing the energies and modifying the activities of the established Congregational churches.

THE CLERGY OF LITCHFIELD COUNTY

It is said that when Stephen Smith Nelson was ordained in 1798 as the first pastor of the first Baptist church in Hartford, he was up to that time the only Baptist minister in Connecticut with a college education.

The Rev. Daniel Wildman, who preached as a licentiate at Plymouth, Connecticut, from 1791 to 1796, and afterward gained a larger reputation in work outside the county, was the earliest preacher of his denomination in this county to achieve mention in Sprague's "Annals."

The Rev. Rufus Babcock was a man whose name has a commanding place in our history. He was a soldier in the War of the Revolution, and belonged to the Separate Congregational Church in Canaan. He became a Baptist preacher and gathered a church in Colebrook, Connecticut, where he was ordained in 1794, the first minister of any denomination settled in that town. He later organized a church in another part of the town, also one in Winsted, and one in the Newfield parish of Torrington. He continued to serve his first parish, with excursions outside, until seventy-three years of age. He baptized more than five hundred members, some say a thousand. He supported his family mainly by farming, and sent two sons to Brown University. One of these sons, the Rev. Rufus Babcock, D.D., was recognized as a leading man in his denomination.

Rufus Babcock, Jr., was born in Colebrook, Septem-

BAPTISTS

ber 19, 1798, was brought up on his father's farm, and graduated from Brown University in 1821. In the same year he became tutor in the Columbian College at Washington, D. C. In 1823 he was ordained pastor of the Baptist Church in Poughkeepsie, New York. In 1826 he became pastor in Salem, Massachusetts, and in 1833 President of Waterville College in Maine. While in that position he was given the degree of D.D. by Bowdoin College. He was afterward offered the presidency of three other colleges or universities, but declined. He was for many years President of the American Baptist Publication Society, and the Corresponding Secretary of the American and Foreign Bible Society. He, as friend and pastor of Matthew Vassar, was consulted about the plans for Vassar College and assisted in its organization. He was the author of several volumes, and a frequent contributor to the press. Toward the close of his life, when he had retired from his larger work, he returned to Colebrook and took up the pastorate of the Baptist church which his father had founded, and which had become weak. He died at Salem, Massachusetts, May 4, 1875, in the seventy-seventh year of his age. He left two daughters.

The following estimate of his character is from the Rev. F. B. Wheeler of Poughkeepsie: "Affectionate and sunny in his disposition, all were won to him; courteous and gentlemanly in his bearing, all respected him; a man

THE CLERGY OF LITCHFIELD COUNTY

of warm Christian spirit, all revered him. His memory is precious in many hearts. He was preëminently a peacemaker, always ready to conciliate and turn away wrath. . . . As a preacher he was a positive power in his denomination, persuasive in oratory and thoroughly evangelical in his doctrine. While he was warmly attached to the principles and faith of the Baptist Church, there was no narrowness in his spirit, but a catholicity of feeling and action that was delightfully refreshing to all with whom he came in contact. Honored by his brethren and his church, he has entered into rest, like a shock of corn fully ripe into the garner."

Another Baptist minister who belonged especially to Colebrook, the Rev. Amos Benedict, seems to me worthy of special mention. He looked temporarily after the interests of several of the smaller churches of his denomination in this county, but was more widely known as a lecturer, especially on temperance. He was a man of brilliant parts, of catholic spirit, and possessed a large fund of miscellaneous knowledge. He has rested from labor but a little while and is remembered by many with affection and reverence.

In the last generation Baptist churches have been established in most of our large villages. They are cared for by pastors of college training and splendid abilities, some of them making history for the future, and who would demand mention here if we were deal-

BAPTISTS

ing with living men rather than seeking to preserve memories of the past. I have no doubt that the earlier men, whose names and lives I have not been able to set forth adequately, were in fact a very essential and valuable factor in the religious development of the county. Criticism of the established churches was constantly needed, and was a stimulus to their activities. A zealous class of workers among the least educated or poorer people brings to pass a new and more emotional as well as less conventional range of religious experience, that in itself is a genuine testimony to the reality of the divine inworking in all men. These earlier Baptist evangelists were in large measure superseded by the Methodist itinerants, working with the same methods but more systematically; as they in turn, after a period of education and culture, were followed by the Adventists, and more recently by the Salvation Army. The great work is one, but the workers need to be of varied gifts, and a large range of thinking as well as of working helps bring the victorious establishment of the great kingdom of truth and righteousness.

CHAPTER XII

THE METHODISTS

HE latest attack in great force on the old order of things came from the Methodists. Their work in Litchfield County practically began with the nineteenth century, and when once begun, it brought to pass great and rapid changes. The Methodist movement had energy, an effective system of organization, and an aggressiveness that seized on every point of vantage. The Baptists had accepted the old theology, and made their contests on the one matter of baptism. Their work in the outside districts made converts, but the disaffected Congregationalists were not always attracted to immersion and often *did* wish their children baptized. The Methodist preacher had all the gifts that appealed to the uneducated, allowed liberty in the

Methodist Episcopal Church, Winsted

THE METHODISTS

matter of baptism, opposed the method of supporting the clergy by taxes, and attacked Calvinism itself with a zeal that never flagged. In a little time they largely superseded the earlier Baptist churches, though the first Methodism was a matter of ministers rather than of churches. Classes were formed wherever converts were made, which met in private houses, and the organization of churches could wait.

In 1789 Jesse Lee took charge of all New England, which up to that time had no Methodist church or minister. He soon had seven men traveling and preaching from Maine to New York.

In 1793 Daniel Ostrander was sent to the Litchfield circuit and preached far and wide from Litchfield as a center. He continued to preach for about fifty years and became a presiding elder, but I think his work in this county was limited to a few months in the beginning of his ministry, when he was about twenty-one years of age.

In 1794 Enoch Mudge preached once around the Litchfield circuit. He was afterward prominent in Maine and Massachusetts. Billy Hibbard took the circuit in 1798 and again in 1815. At the first appointment he had already been preaching a year and was about twenty-six years old. In his second turn he was contemporary with Dr. Lyman Beecher, with whom he was on most friendly terms. He was a chaplain in the army in

THE CLERGY OF LITCHFIELD COUNTY

1814, and in his later years lived in Canaan, Connecticut. He was a man of influence and power.

Freeborn Garretson seems to have been the man who gave special impetus to early Methodism in this section of the country. He was presiding elder in the New York Conference in 1791, 1797, 1800–1803, and 1811–1814. In this office he looked after the interests of western Connecticut and eastern New York. He was a large-minded man who aimed in a statesmanlike way at the establishment of Christianity rather than the success of a denomination, but none the less was loyal and successful in his denominational work. He tried to build up his churches from the elements not already gathered into organized churches, rather than to make division or weaken the forces already at work for the salvation of men. It was hardly possible, however, in those days for a Methodist minister to preach a sermon without directly controverting doctrines taught in the established churches, and it was a matter of conscience to do it thoroughly. From his day the Methodist churches were a permanent factor in the religious development of Litchfield County. The preachers began their work at an earlier age than the pastors of Congregational churches, and usually without a college education or special theological training. They learned to preach by preaching, and learned their theology while they were preaching it. They appealed to the neglected

THE METHODISTS

classes, and called into action an emotional type of religion, which made up in energy for lack of scholarship. The kind of work which conditions forced upon them broke the trammels of conventionality, and promoted genuineness in thinking and religious experience until a new type of conventionality was formed. The emphasis they laid on free will and human activity went to an extreme beyond the teaching of their own greatest theologians, and was a constant challenge to the old theology, which ascribed all possibility or actual attainment of goodness wholly to the immediate act and eternal plan of God himself. In this way controversy for the first half of the nineteenth century came to hold a chief interest in the preaching alike in the old church and in the new. The itinerant system prevented the identification of individual ministers for the most part with anything so small as a county. Under supervision from a central authority, men were constantly changing their field of work and so enlarging their experience and interests that the church as a whole rather than the demands of separate localities occupied their minds. Each year brought a new minister, continuing without break the plan of his predecessors, and preparing the way for another to follow. Hence, while the impact of Methodist preaching was with power and wrought great changes, and many of their preachers were men of mark, their work was more productive of conformity to the

THE CLERGY OF LITCHFIELD COUNTY

outside world than of the distinctive characteristics which connotate the development of local history.

Great men there were and long remembered, preaching for a year in a dozen places, perhaps wholly in the county, probably some of them outside, and then for forty or fifty years devoting themselves to similar work elsewhere. Great as were the names they made, and effective as the team-work might be in which they had a part, it is difficult to find out and put on record the part which as individuals they had in the history of Litchfield County.

The Rev. Daniel Smith was born in Salisbury, Connecticut, in 1806. He began to preach on the Goshen circuit in 1830, and was stationed in Winsted in 1834 and 1835. He was a writer of Sunday-school books and a lecturer of some ability.

The influence of the Methodist preachers in changing the prevalent Calvinistic theology was wrought not only by their own direct teaching, but by the change of attitude necessitated in the Congregational pastors who preached in defense of their own doctrines. A wise man with a position to defend may change the position altogether in making it defensible. Dr. Lyman Beecher, Dr. Nathaniel Taylor, and others of their time used to insist that they held loyally to all the essentials of the older New England theology. They only improved the statement of it to guard against misapprehensions and

THE METHODISTS

misrepresentations. None the less, when they got through, we had entered a new world of religious thought and activity. How much the Methodist preachers had to do with the newer thinking, we do not know, and it is not necessary to know, but they had their part, and many factors coöperated. The coming of railroads, telegraphs, and telephones has done away with the separateness of the Litchfield County people.

New people and new races are here. Not only the older churches have been modified in character and belief; Methodism itself has equally changed. Her churches also demand ministers of liberal education, and their members adopt the ways of the world. Adventism took up for a time the work among the uneducated, and has been followed by the Salvation Army. Individual and local peculiarities still have their occasional distinction, and old prejudices or opinions are sometimes appealed to and momentarily revived, but in the main we are swept by the current of movements that are worldwide. The attempt has been made in these papers to recall as fairly as possible some of the special phases of a past time that may be worth remembering. It is too much for the present writer to presume to measure the present or to prophesy concerning the future. The shortcomings in these studies are evident, but the labor has been one of love, and the reader's forgiveness is hoped for.

THE CLERGY OF LITCHFIELD COUNTY

PREACHERS

FOLLOWING is a list of the preachers who have labored in Winsted and vicinity from 1790 to 1903:

LITCHFIELD CIRCUIT

1790 Samuel Wigton and Henry Christie.
1791 Mathias Swain and James Covel.
1792 Philip Wager and James Coleman.
1793 Samuel Smith and Daniel Ostrander.
1794 Fredus Aldridge and James Covel.
1795 Jesse Stoneman and Joseph Mitchell.
1796 Daniel Dennis and Wesley Budd.
1797 Ezekiel Canfield and William Thatcher.
1798 Ebenezer Stevens and Truman Bishop.
1799 Augustus Jocelyn.
1800 Aaron Hunt and Elijah Batchelor.
1801 Peter Moriarty and John Sweet.
1802 James Campbell and Luman Andrus.
1803 Caleb Morris and John Sweet.
1804 Zalmon Lyon and Ebben Smith.
1805 Zalmon Lyon.
1806 Nathan Emory and Samuel Corcoran.
1807 Aaron Hunt and Jonathan Lyon.
1808 Henry Eames and Andrew Prindle.
1809–10 Laban Clark and Reuben Harris.
1811 James Covel and Arnold Scofield.
1812 James Coleman and Benjamin Griffin.
1813 William Swazey, Gad Smith, and Jonathan Reynolds.
1814 William Swazey, Thomas Thorp, and Jonathan Reynolds.
1815 Samuel Corcoran, Billy Hibbard, and Smith Dayton.

THE METHODISTS

BURLINGTON CIRCUIT

1816 Phineas Cook and Aaron Pierce.
1818 Phineas Cook and Cyrus Culver.
1818-19 Nathaniel Emory and Cyrus Silliman.
1820 Datus Ensign and Nathan Ruggles.
1821 Datus Ensign and Julius Field.
1822 Cyrus Silliman and John Luckey.
1823 Henry Hatfield and Stephen L. Stillman.
1824 Samuel D. Ferguson and Julius Field.
1825 Samuel D. Ferguson and Elbert Osborn.
1826 Joseph McRerey and Elbert Osborn.
1827 Gershom Pierce and Wells Wolcott.
1828 Aaron Pierce and L. Baldwin.
1829 Aaron Pierce and L. Mead.
1830 Quartus Stewart and L. Mead.
1831 Quartus Stewart and Philo Ferris.
1832 Charles Sherman and C. W. Turner.
1833 Charles Sherman and John Nixon.

STATIONED PREACHERS

	YEARS		YEARS
1834 Daniel Smith, first stationed preacher	2	1845 W. H. Ferris	2
		1847 Seymour Landon	1
1836 Thomas Bainbridge	2	1848 Harvey Husted	2
1838 Joseph Law	1	1850 Albert Nash	2
1839 Davis Stocking	2	1852 George W. Woodruff	2
1841 Ebenezer Washburn	2	1854 John Crawford	1
1843 D. W. Clark	2	1855 S. A. Seaman	2

THE CLERGY OF LITCHFIELD COUNTY
STATIONED PREACHERS—Continued

	YEARS		YEARS
1857 Otis Saxton	2	1877 W. H. Thomas	2
1859 W. T. Hill	2	1879 Joseph Pullman	3
1861 Reuben Loomis	2	1882 I. E. Smith	3
1863 L. W. Abbott	2	1885 T. C. Beach	3
1865 S. H. Platt	3	1888 J. Rippers	4
1868 B. Pillisbury	1	1892 A. H. Wyatt	1
1869 W. H. Simonson	3	1893 D. A. Jordan	1
1872 A. Graves	2	1894 E. S. Ferry	5
1874 B. T. Abbott	3	1899–1909 B. F. Kidder	11

PRESIDING ELDERS

1790 Freeborn Garretson
1791 Jesse Lee
1792 Jacob Brush
1793 George Roberts
1794 Jesse Lee
1795 Freeborn Garretson
1796 Sylvester Hutchinson
1797 Freeborn Garretson
1798–9 Sylvester Hutchinson
1800–2 Freeborn Garretson
1803–5 Daniel Ostrander
1806–7 Peter Moriarty
1808–10 Aaron Hunt
1811 William Anson
1812 Elijah Woolsey
1813–16 Nathan Bangs
1817–20 Ebenezer Washburn

1821–23 Samuel Merwin
1824–26 Samuel Luckey
1827 Arnold Scofield
1828–31 Laban Clark
1832 Heman Bangs
1833–36 Stephen Martindale
1837–40 Laban Clark
1841–42 Samuel D. Ferguson
1843–47 Bartholomew Creagh
1848–51 Seymour Landon
1852–54 John B. Stratton
1855 D. Miller (died)
       L. C. Cheney
1856–61 E. C. Griswold
1862–63 W. C. Hoyt
1864 Thomas G. Osborn
1865–68 Nathaniel Mead

THE METHODISTS
PRESIDING ELDERS—Continued

1869–71 T. C. Osborn
1872–75 M. L. Scudder
1876 G. A. Hubbell
1877–79 W. T. Hill
1880–83 G. A. Hubbell

1884–87 W. H. Wardell
1888–92 John W. Beach
1893–98 Crandall J. North
1899–1902 John E. Adams
1903 W. A. Richard

CHAPTER XIII

THE CLERGY AS CITIZENS

IGH and holy as the minister was once held in popular esteem, he was not shut out by his sanctity from participation in all that concerned the common life and common interests of the people. He was usually regarded as the first citizen in the community. He gave advice either in his private capacity or formally from the pulpit in regard to the conduct of affairs in town or State. This grew out of the fact that New England was settled with the religious motive dominant, in the hope of establishing a Christian nation, governed in accordance with Christian principles.

This leadership of the clergy was promotive of good order and high ideals. As two political parties grew up for organized conflict, there also came to pass, naturally,

Congregational Church, East Canaan

THE CLERGY AS CITIZENS

a division in which the ministers and leading church members were massed on one side, and all irreligious elements on the other. This had its unfortunate bearing on the development of society, creating with some a political bias against religious influences, and also sometimes tending to commit the ministers and churches to judgment in favor of class interests rather than to an equal regard for all the people. That is, ministers dealing with the affairs of the public were constantly liable to look at measures from the side of a privileged class, and so with the best of intentions failed to do equal justice to all.

Notwithstanding mistakes and difficulties the leading of the clergy, or their criticism of public affairs, has been greatly helpful to public progress in right directions.

Litchfield County ministers have, as a matter of course, been leaders in education. They have been first in establishing schools of all grades. From the beginning they selected and examined teachers and superintended their work. They either organized academies or themselves prepared young people for college, and were influential in inspiring them to seek a college course. Their preaching in itself has been educational. They have helped in forming libraries and promoting a reading habit and social methods of literary culture. In patriotism they have never been lacking. Before the

THE CLERGY OF LITCHFIELD COUNTY

War of the Revolution sermons were preached in most of the churches, and resolutions were passed by ministerial associations, asserting the rights of the people and arousing them to maintain their liberties.

The Rev. Judah Champion of Litchfield, the Rev. Cotton Mather Smith of Sharon, and the Rev. Ammi Ruhamah Robbins of Norfolk, in addition to their patriotic preaching, went as chaplains in the Revolutionary army. As I have referred to this in other chapters, I will not enlarge upon it here, except to quote from Mr. Champion's sermon of May, 1776, from Gal. v. 1: "Methinks we may this day well-nigh see the ghosts of our departed progenitors, and hear those blessed worthies, in solemn accents, through the vast of heaven, addressing us, saying, 'Stand fast in the liberty wherewith Christ hath made you free.' At the inestimable price of his blood, the glorious Redeemer purchased these blessings for his people. Through rivers of blood and tribulation we have been made the instruments of handing them down to you. Nor can you wantonly throw them away without incurring Jehovah's indignation and curse. Trust in God and firmly defy every danger. Heaven demands your most vigorous exertions." These accounts are preserved in "Centennial Papers of the General Conference of Connecticut," published in Hartford in 1877, and may be found quoted in various periodicals.

THE CLERGY AS CITIZENS

The Rev. Publius Vergilius Bogue, pastor at Winchester from 1790 to 1800, served in the war as a soldier, as did the Rev. Rufus Babcock, founder of the Baptist churches in Colebrook, and others who were afterward ministers in our churches. The War of 1812 and the war with Mexico were not much favored by the ministers and churches of New England, and I do not know of any patriotic enthusiasm shown in regard to these wars by the Congregational clergy of Litchfield County. But Billy Hibbard was chaplain in the War of 1812-14. In the Civil War of 1861-1865, the Rev. Hiram Eddy, D.D., pastor at Winsted, went as chaplain, as did the Rev. Henry Upson of New Preston, and the Rev. John B. Doolittle, afterward pastor at Bridgewater. The Rev. Isaac P. Powell, later pastor at North Canaan, was an officer in the army, and by his experience in a rebel prison was much broken in health. The Rev. John F. Gleason served in the army and was afterward pastor at Norfolk.

The temperance reformation at the beginning of the nineteenth century owed much to the ministers of Litchfield County. A sermon by the Rev. Ebenezer Porter, D.D., when pastor at Washington, Connecticut, in 1806, was marked in its influence and was used for many years as a temperance tract. The beginning of an organized campaign against intemperance got its impetus from Dr. Lyman Beecher at Litchfield. His account of the drink-

THE CLERGY OF LITCHFIELD COUNTY

ing customs of the day as he found them in use at the meetings of ministers and churches of his time gives us a view of the situation which aroused him to action. In his Autobiography, page 245, we read: "September 6, 1810. Well, at the ordination at Plymouth, the preparation for our creature comforts, beside food, was a broad sideboard covered with decanters and bottles and sugar and pitchers of water. There we found all the kinds of liquor then in vogue. The drinking was apparently universal. . . . When the consociation arrived, they always took something to drink around; also before public services, and always on their return. There was a decanter of spirits also on the dinner-table, and gentlemen partook of it during the afternoon and evening if they felt the need; and the sideboard looked and smelled like the bar of a very active grog-shop. When they had all done drinking, and had taken pipes and tobacco, in less than fifteen minutes there was such a smoke you could n't see. And the noise I cannot describe; it was the maximum of hilarity. They told their stories and were at the height of jocose talk. . . . The next ordination was of Mr. Harvey in Goshen (October, 1810), and there was the same preparation, the same scenes, and then afterward still louder murmurs from the society at the quantity and expense of liquors consumed. . . . The two meetings were near together, and in both, my alarm, shame, and indignation were intense.

[174]

THE CLERGY AS CITIZENS

... And silently I took an oath before God that I would never attend another ordination of that kind."

The next year, 1811, the General Association appointed a committee to make inquiries. At their report in Sharon in 1812, the committee stated that an alarming condition existed, but they could see no way out of it. Dr. Beecher at once moved that a committee of three be appointed immediately to report at the same meeting something to be done. He was made chairman of the committee, and the report was in part as follows:

"The General Association of Connecticut, taking into consideration the undue consumption of ardent spirits, the enormous sacrifice of property resulting, the alarming increase of intemperance, the deadly effect on health, intellect, the family, society, civil and religious institutions, and especially in nullifying the means of grace and destroying souls, recommend:

"1. Appropriate discourses on the subject by all ministers of the Association.

"2. That district associations abstain from the use of ardent spirits at ecclesiastical meetings.

"3. That members of churches abstain from the unlawful vending, or purchase and use of ardent spirits, where unlawfully sold; exercise vigilant discipline, and cease to consider the production of ardent spirits a part of hospitable entertainment in social visits."

Similar action was urged upon the various district

associations throughout the State and was generally adopted by them. Dr. Beecher also worked successfully for laws restricting saloons. In 1826 he preached a series of six sermons on the nature, signs, evils, and remedies of intemperance, which were published and widely circulated. Most of the Congregational ministers in the State soon became total abstainers. The work thus begun took on a wider range than abstaining from intoxicating liquors. The Connecticut Society for the Reformation of Morals also opposed gambling, lottery-dealing, and Sabbath-breaking. Dr. Beecher and others in the county were also vigorous preachers against slavery and its political aggressions in the nation.

The late Benjamin Mead Wright, when pastor in Kent, was successful in rousing the public opinion of several towns in the Housatonic Valley against bribery in elections, and was the means of introducing a Corrupt Practices Bill into the Connecticut Legislature, which prepared the way for our present law. Our ministers have not been politicians in the usual sense of the term, but they have kept a diligent outlook toward all questions affecting the common interests and the public morals, and have been quick to respond to all wise attempts for promoting the cause of righteousness or the uplifting of men.

CHAPTER XIV

THE CLERGY IN LITERATURE

EN in the strenuous life, struggling either for their own existence or for some greater purpose, are not likely to make great achievements in art or culture. Litchfield County is justly proud of her great men and women and of the work they have done for the world. She has given worthy contributions to literature, but in this does not claim a special eminence. The ministers of her earlier history had, as we have seen, a predominant influence along the lines of their own work. They were thorough in their preaching and teaching, and their published writings mainly extended and emphasized the power of their pulpits.

Dr. Joseph Bellamy was known throughout the English-speaking world by the most popular religious work of his day, "True Religion Delineated," which had a large sale on both sides of the Atlantic. In his later life

THE CLERGY OF LITCHFIELD COUNTY

he published several controversial pamphlets. These, with a few sermons preached on special occasions, were collected and edited by a former pupil, the Rev. Noah Benedict of Woodbury, and published, with a sketch of his life, in three good-sized volumes, which are still accessible to students. His successor in Bethlehem, the Rev. Azel Backus, D.D., has left us a volume of sermons.

The Rev. Nathaniel William Taylor, D.D., of New Milford and New Haven, has given us several volumes in theology: "Practical Sermons," "Lectures on Moral Government," "Essays," "Lectures on Selected Topics of Revealed Theology." His son-in-law, the Rev. Noah Porter, D.D., LL.D., pastor at New Milford and President of Yale College, was the author of many valuable works which had a place both in science and literature. The Rev. Ebenezer Porter, D.D., pastor in Washington, Connecticut, from 1796 to 1812, and born in Cornwall, Connecticut, October 5, 1772, published among other books: "Letters on Religious Revivals," "Lectures on Eloquence and Style," "The Rhetorical Reader" (a book much used in higher schools), and "Sermons."

The Rev. Leonard E. Lathrop, pastor in Salisbury from 1825 to 1836, published a volume of sermons on "The Nature and Influence of Evangelical Faith." The Rev. Jonathan Edwards, D.D., first pastor at Colebrook, was the author of volumes of sermons and theo-

THE CLERGY IN LITERATURE

logical treatises which were an essential part of the theological development of New England. His successor, the Rev. Chauncey Lee, D.D., pastor at Colebrook from 1800 to 1828, published a volume of sermons, accompanied by one of original hymns written for use with the sermons. He was also the author of a metrical translation of the Book of Job, as an epic poem entitled "The Trial of Virtue," which in its day was popular and had a wide circulation. The Rev. Thomas Robbins, D.D., who was a pretty good authority on books, says of it in his diary, "I think it one of the best poems ever published in this country."

A third Colebrook pastor, the Rev. Edward Royal Tyler, was afterward for a time editor of the *Connecticut Observer* at Hartford. Later he became the first editor and part proprietor of the *New Englander*. He wrote many valuable articles for this review. He published a book on Future Punishment, and a Congregational Handbook or Catechism. His work was carried on under continual burdens of ill health and shortened by early death.

Dr. Lyman Beecher of Litchfield, as well as nearly all his children, were large contributors to the literature of the nation. Their work is too well known to call for enumeration. Dr. Charles G. Finney, of Warren and Oberlin, has enriched theological literature by his Autobiography and his published sermons. Dr. Edward

THE CLERGY OF LITCHFIELD COUNTY

Dorr Griffin, pastor at New Hartford and President of Williams College, has given us several volumes of sermons and lectures.

Perhaps the most distinguished in poetry and lighter literature of the Litchfield County clergy was the Rev. John Pierpont. He was born in Litchfield South Farms, now Morris, April 6, 1785, studied in Morris Academy, was graduated at Yale in 1804, and studied law at the Litchfield Law School. He was variously lawyer, business man, clergyman, statistician, poet, mechanical inventor, and popular lecturer. As a clergyman he was Unitarian, Orthodox, and Spiritualist. He died at Medford, Massachusetts, August 27, 1866. In 1816 he published a volume of poetry under the title "Airs of Palestine," which was republished with his other poems in 1840. His name is not often mentioned among the literary celebrities of New England, but he had a wide reputation in his own generation, and left behind poems which are worth remembering. One, commemorating a son that died, is among the best of its kind, and is, I suppose, well known, beginning:

> I cannot make him dead:
> His fair sunshiny head
> Is ever bounding round my study chair;
> Yet, when my eyes, now dim
> With tears, I turn to him,
> The vision vanishes—he is not there.

Charles G. Finney

THE CLERGY IN LITERATURE

His ode on the Pilgrim Fathers, written for a celebration at Plymouth, December 22, 1824, was worthy of the occasion. A poem called "Passing Away" seems to me beautiful. The present writer remembers him as a speaker at a Yale alumni meeting, giving some personal reminiscences of Abraham Lincoln. The following description is taken from an article by John Neal in the *Atlantic Monthly* for December, 1866: "He was tall, straight, and spare, six feet I should say, and rather ungraceful in fact, though called by the women of his parish not only the most graceful, but the most finished of gentlemen. That he was dignified, courteous, and prepossessing, very pleasant in conversation, a capital story-teller, I am ready to acknowledge, but he wanted ease of manner. . . . His tall figure, his erect, positive bearing, and somewhat uncompromising, severe expression of countenance, when much in earnest, with black heavy eyebrows, clear blue eyes which passed for black, and stiff black hair, were all of the Huguenot Southern type. . . . I was constantly reminded of John C. Calhoun, a fellow-student with him at Yale."

Dr. Horace Bushnell not only wrought a great change in the theological world by his thinking, but was master in the use of language. In sermons, theological and philosophical treatises, he took a commanding place in literature.

Samuel J. Andrews, D.D., son of the Rev. William

THE CLERGY OF LITCHFIELD COUNTY

Andrews of Cornwall, and licensed by the Litchfield North Association, was the author of a "Life of Christ" that has been highly valued by scholars for a generation. The Rev. Lavalette Perrin, D.D., was for several years editor of the *Religious Herald* of Hartford, and maintained it in a high degree of excellence. The Rev. D. D. T. McLaughlin, of Sharon, Litchfield, and Morris, was a man of literary tastes, and devoted his leisure for many years to a new lyrical translation of the Psalms, intended to preserve the special qualities of their Hebrew style. Sorrow at the loss of his son prevented him from securing their publication in book form before his own death.

Two volumes of selected sermons were published by a committee of ministers in this vicinity, one in 1798, the other in 1810. They are of special historic interest to the people of Litchfield County. Many sermons and religious articles from the ministers of this county found their way into the *National Preacher,* the *Connecticut Evangelical Magazine,* and the *Christian Spectator.* It is unfortunate that writers for the last two magazines were accustomed to use pseudonyms, so that it is difficult in many cases to identify them.

The Rev. Thomas Robbins, D.D., a son of the Norfolk pastor, and preacher for a year and three months in Winchester, besides having much to do with our churches in many ways, collected a series of his articles from the

THE CLERGY IN LITERATURE

Evangelical Magazine, and published them in 1815 in a book entitled "Historic View of the Early Planters of New England." His greatest contribution to literature was in his diary, which was published after his death by his nephew, the Hon. Robbins Battell. The ministers of the present generation are somewhat given to authorship; in fact, one is hardly considered in good standing until he has published a book. To the prevalence of such a custom may be attributed the ambition of the present writer to attempt an invasion into literature. It has been the purpose of this book to avoid speaking of living men, but simply to enumerate some of the literary work done by men of our time can hardly be objectionable.

Some of our ministers have contributed works on local history. The late Rev. Samuel Wolcott Orcutt published, among other books, a "History of Torrington," having been for a time pastor of the First Church in that town. The Rev. Augustine G. Hibbard gave us an excellent history of Goshen. The Rev. Giles F. Goodenough is the author of "Gossip about a Country Parish, being a History of Ellsworth Parish in the Town of Sharon." The Rev. Wesley E. Page for Milton, and the Rev. Gerald Stanley Lee for Sharon, have contributed pamphlets.

Perhaps because problems of morals and theology are not so urgently demanding solution as in the earlier

THE CLERGY OF LITCHFIELD COUNTY

times, our clergy take a wider range in their literary work, give more attention to lighter themes, and aim at a more artistic finish. The Rev. Gerald Stanley Lee, formerly pastor at Sharon, besides books like "The Shadow-Christ," containing word-pictures of spiritual visions, has written many essays of a critical character. The Rev. John Sheridan Zelie, in younger days pastor in Plymouth, is a contributor to periodical literature in similar ways. The Rev. John Calvin Goddard of Salisbury has published "Leaves of Absence, and Other Leaves," and is constantly bringing the public under new obligations. The Rev. Edward O. Dyer, pastor at Sharon from 1893 to 1906, is the author of "Gnadensee." The Rev. Herbert K. Job, pastor in Kent, is the author of several well-known books about birds. The Rev. Myron M. Munson, lately of Warren, has a book on the genealogy of the Munson family. The Rev. Thomas C. Richards, of Winsted and Torrington, now pastor in Warren, Massachusetts, is the author of one of the leading missionary biographies of the present day, "Samuel J. Mills, Missionary Pathfinder." The Rev. Newell M. Calhoun, born in Bethlehem, pastor for ten years in Winsted, Fellow of Yale University, has two books to his credit, "Litchfield County Sketches" and "Picturesque Litchfield County." The Rev. A. W. Ackerman, D.D., of the Center Church, Torrington, has written a story of Old Testament times, entitled

THE CLERGY IN LITERATURE

"The Price of Peace, or A Story of the Times of Ahab, King of Israel."

That this list is not longer is probably due more to lack of information than to lack of material, and will call out testimony from others to make good the deficiency.

CHAPTER XV

WIT AND HUMOR

ERSONAL peculiarities and eccentricities have sometimes characterized men who find their way into the pulpit, as well as those in more secular occupations. In such cases the conception of solemnity and dignity associated with the ministry has given special emphasis to that which was peculiar and personal. Flashes of light from a dark cloud attract attention.

I shall not attempt to make a careful distinction between wit and humor, but assume that there is a recognized difference, passing through many gradations, between the sharpness of mind which is a ready weapon in controversy or repartee, and the large-hearted good nature which lives in the sunshine and consciously or unconsciously reflects warmth and glory on all around. The narrow and ignorant may possess the power of ridi-

WIT AND HUMOR

cule and stinging retort; only the larger-minded who see men and things from more than one side have the capacity for humor as well as wit, and the ability to use both effectively for the best service of mankind instead of merely for triumph in a personal argument.

There have been many of the ministers in Litchfield County eminent in the use of wit and humor. It would not be wise to enter into extensive detail with regard to the pastors who in almost every community have left behind them traditions of characteristic peculiarity or smartness in retort or repartee. Most of the jokes handed down have been sufficiently repeated to be pretty well known or easily accessible, and some of them are fickle and have the habit of attaching themselves to different persons.

In reading some of the old sermons or studying the accepted belief of the early preachers, it might seem impossible that men who felt the responsibility of such belief and such preaching could ever have smiled, but God has so constituted our human nature that it seeks relief and finds it. If this relief comes through inconsistencies and incongruities, it makes a happy excuse for the inconsistencies. The custom of sharp contests of wit in social intercourse seems to have been cultivated by our forefathers, and if it was often the cause of coarseness and buffoonery among the common people, among the better educated it rose into the higher atmosphere of brilliancy,

THE CLERGY OF LITCHFIELD COUNTY

though sometimes of a rather stiff or stilted character. John Trumbull of Watertown, Dr. Bellamy of Bethlehem, and still more his successor, Dr. Azel Backus, were remembered for their sharp sayings. It became so natural to Dr. Backus to give witty turns to his speech that he was unable wholly to repress it in his preaching.

Of course this, from the professional point of view, was greatly to be regretted. Great as was the personal dignity and authority of the minister among the people, the pulpit itself and the clergyman in the pulpit had an added sacredness. If the minister's human nature might be allowed some relief at an appropriate time and place, there was great danger in permitting the people to relax from the solemnity of the Lord's house and the responsibility of divine service.

Even Dr. Chauncey Lee of Colebrook, renowned for his wit and merriment on social occasions, was, I think, never accused of carrying his humor into the pulpit.

There were, however, men in those days who, in a way natural to themselves, carried not only wit but humor into their pulpit ministrations without detriment to the deep spiritual force of their influence. Such men were the Rev. Ammi Robbins of Norfolk, Samuel J. Mills of Torringford, and Lemuel Haynes of Torrington. I have been told that it was the usual custom of Father Mills to introduce a pleasant story or witticism when the people showed signs of weariness or inattention

WIT AND HUMOR

in the middle of a sermon, for the express purpose of giving his congregation a needed rest and so securing better attention to what he wished to say further. The sketch of his life given earlier in this book sufficiently illustrates his habit and its success.

Dr. Farrand's wit was of that sarcastic kind which would naturally give an added sting and force to many things in his preaching, and could probably have been brought into service many times when his sense of what the pulpit required kept him under restraint. The story is told of him, in the memoir of the Rev. Lemuel Haynes, that he was walking with a rich neighbor, who with considerable pride called his attention to the richness of the farm he owned, and the value of a beautiful brook flowing through it. Mr. Farrand replied by quoting at once the following verse of a hymn:

> Though a broad stream, with golden sands,
> Through all his meadows roll,
> Yet he's a wretch, with all his lands,
> Who wears a narrow soul.

"While riding with a young clergyman, he beheld, at a little distance from the highway, two or three Indians at their work; and turning, rode up and gave them an affectionate salutation. After overtaking his fellow-traveler, he received a sharp rebuke for his attention to the Indians. He replied, 'They always treat me with

THE CLERGY OF LITCHFIELD COUNTY

good manners when I meet them, and I should be ashamed to have it said that the minister of the parish has n't as good manners as an Indian.'"

One of the most marked examples of eccentricity and wit was the Rev. Lemuel Haynes. He was a mulatto and was abandoned by his parents when an infant. He was born at West Hartford, Connecticut, July 18, 1753. At the age of five months he was bound out to Deacon David Rose of Granville, Massachusetts. Having been sent to school long enough to learn to read, he studied evenings in the chimney-corner such books as he could get. In this way he learned by heart large portions of the Scripture, Watts' Hymns and Psalms, Young's "Night Thoughts," and Doddridge's Works. One of his sayings was, "I make it my rule to know something more every night than I knew in the morning." After reaching manhood he studied Latin with Dr. Farrand in Canaan, working on the farm to pay his way. He then learned Greek in a similar way, and began to preach at the age of twenty-seven. He first served as a soldier in the Revolutionary War.

He preached successfully in Torrington from 1786 to 1789. He drew large congregations, notwithstanding his color. It is said of one man that he refused to attend for some time until curiosity prevailed over prejudice. He took his seat in the crowded church, but purposely kept his hat on. "The preacher had not gone far in his

WIT AND HUMOR

sermon," said the man, "before I thought him the whitest man I ever saw. My hat was taken off and thrown under the seat, and I found myself listening with the most profound attention." He became a man of prayer and piety.

Mr. Haynes had a vivid and terse way of putting his statements. I have never seen the usual argument for an accepted doctrine of Calvinism more plausibly stated than in one of his sermons: "Does God give a sinner a new heart to-day? All say that he is good for this act. If God formed the design of saving that sinner one day beforehand, he was good during a whole day for such a design. What if God determined from eternity to sanctify that sinner? Then he was eternally good for such a determination. This is God's decree of election; therefore, his eternally electing love, instead of proving that he is a hard Master, proves his eternal, unchangeable goodness."

Some of his students went to him to complain of having been slandered, expecting sympathy. He merely replied, "I knew all this before." "Why, then," said one, "did you not inform us?" "Because," said he, "it was not worth telling; and I now tell you plainly and once for all, it is best to let the devil carry his own mail and bear its expenses."

"Mr. Haynes was a strong advocate for an educated ministry, and often expressed his regret at his own lack.

THE CLERGY OF LITCHFIELD COUNTY

A young clergyman remarked on one occasion that ministers without learning succeeded well, and that often ignorant ones did best. 'Won't you tell me then,' said Mr. Haynes, 'how much ignorance is necessary to make an eminent preacher?' "

A physician of loose principles whom he had sometimes employed called to take leave of him as he was about to move away. Mr. Haynes said, "I was not aware that you expected to leave this part of the country so soon. I am owing you a small amount, which ought to have been canceled before. I have not the money, but will go and borrow it immediately." The doctor handed him a receipt in full, saying, "Here, Mr. Haynes, is a discharge of your account. You have been a faithful servant here for a long time, and receive but small support; I give you the debt—but, Mr. Haynes, you must pray for me and make me a good man." Mr. Haynes quickly replied, "Why, doctor, I think I had much better pay the debt."

The pastor of a neighboring parish was a confirmed bachelor, and, at the request of some of his people, Mr. Haynes tried to convince him that it would be better to marry. "The clergyman replied that he felt the force of his remarks, and was disposed to think of the subject seriously, adding very emphatically, 'I understand, Mr. Haynes, that you have some very fine daughters.' Mr. Haynes instantly replied, 'I have sympathy for you and

Austin Isham

your parishioners; but, really, I have taken great pains to educate my daughters, and much care to prepare them for usefulness, and I hate to throw them away.' "

Dr. Lyman Beecher and his sons had a saving sense of humor, and a ready wit which was often made to serve a useful purpose. It is said that the doctor was making a call in a neighboring parish, when the lady of the house made some sorrowful criticism of her young pastor, because, while thoroughly good in intention, he lacked the dignity suited to his profession, and among other things was inclined to go fishing, "which," she remarked, "is hardly a respectable thing for a minister." Mr. Beecher jumped up, and addressing a small boy, said, "Bub, go and dig me some worms, and I will make it respectable."

In later times the Rev. Herman L. Vaill, of Litchfield, Milton, and Torringford, the Rev. Austin Isham of Roxbury, and the Rev. Timothy A. Hazen of Goshen, were accustomed to enliven companionship by a flow of witty speech. That any of them purposely introduced humor into the pulpit I do not know. There are living men who are, or have been, pastors in Litchfield County, who are humorists of a high order, and have increased their influence for good by the use of wit even in sermons.

A sense of humor has sustained many a man in trying circumstances and furnished a welcome relief from the continued strain of burdens hard to be borne. Under wise guidance it may give rest to a tired congregation, or awaken their interest in important truth without deflecting their minds from serious thought or high spiritual purpose. It is a valuable gift, but, like all power, has its dangers and needs to be used with caution and restraint.

The present writer recalls six instances in which as many different ministers of this county seriously offended one or more parishioners by attempting a facetious remark. In some cases I have no doubt it shortened the pastorate. "A brother offended is harder to be won than a strong city." If only ministers were to read this book, I should like, for their warning, to recount the six jokes and their effect, but for fear of rekindling old fires I refrain. Ministers of these days, with less of dignity and authority to maintain, have a larger freedom, than of old, to be themselves and to use all their gifts, in the pulpit or out of it; but the very enlargement of liberty carries with it a responsibility for wise caution as well as wise action.

It may show a lack of the humorous sense to turn this chapter into a sermon, but the writer was a preacher before he tried to be a historian.

CHAPTER XVI

MINISTERS' CHILDREN

HERE is an old saying in disparagement of ministers' sons and deacons' daughters, which malicious people like to quote, but the answer is obvious that the children of the clergy usually gain a standing in the world much above the average. One reason for this is probably the fact that Providence furnishes ministers with wives who are usually the best of womankind, and attaches a responsibility to their position specially fitted for the development of sainthood. It seems to me inevitable that some notice should here be given to a few of the best-known men and women who had their birth and upbringing in the families of Litchfield County pastors.

A son of the Rev. John Trumbull of Watertown was

THE CLERGY OF LITCHFIELD COUNTY

the Hon. John Trumbull, LL.D., distinguished both as a learned jurist and as a popular poet. He was born in Watertown, April 24, 1750, and died in Detroit, Michigan, May 12, 1831. At seven years of age he passed the examination for admission to Yale College, but waited six years before entering, graduated at seventeen, and became a tutor at twenty-one. He studied law in the office of John Adams at Boston. He lived for several years in Hartford, was a member of the State Legislature, and from 1801 to 1819 a judge of the Superior Court of Connecticut. His poetical works were published in two volumes. His satirical poem "McFingal" was exceedingly popular and one of the "best sellers" of the time. More than thirty editions were called for. It was written in the style of "Hudibras," and gives a burlesque of the American Revolution, with sketches of particular individuals and characteristic manners, illustrated by humorous incidents.

The Rev. Noah Benedict was ordained pastor in Woodbury, October 22, 1760, and died in the fifty-third year of his pastorate. His son, the Hon. Noah B. Benedict, graduated at Yale in 1788. He was a prominent lawyer in Litchfield County for nearly forty years. He was at various times a member of the upper or lower house of the State Legislature, and for many years a judge of probate in his native town.

The Rev. Daniel Boardman, first pastor at New Mil-

MINISTERS' CHILDREN

ford, has been followed by a long procession of distinguished and useful citizens among his descendants. His son, Colonel Sherman Boardman, was a man of large activity and influence. A grandson, the Hon. Elijah Boardman, was a United States Senator. Another grandson, David L. Boardman, was a lawyer of prominence in the county.

The Rev. Nathaniel Taylor, the second pastor, was equally fortunate in his posterity. The Rev. Nathaniel W. Taylor, D.D., LL.D., was his grandson. He was the leader in the development of the New Haven theology, a theology not well remembered by thinkers of the present day, but in its time a terror to conservative minds and greatly loved by advanced preachers. Other members of the family have been citizens of distinction, whose reputation has reached far beyond the borders of their native town.

The Hon. John Cotton Smith, a son of the Rev. Cotton Mather Smith, was born in Sharon, February 12, 1765. He was graduated at Yale College in 1783, and was admitted to the bar in 1786. He was elected to the State Legislature in 1793, and to the United States Congress in 1800. In 1809 he became a judge of the Supreme Court of Connecticut, was elected Lieutenant Governor in 1811, and Governor in 1813, holding this office until 1817. He was for several years President of the American Board of Commissioners for Foreign

THE CLERGY OF LITCHFIELD COUNTY

Missions and of the American Bible Society. He died December 7, 1845, at nearly eighty-one years of age. Helen Evertson Smith, author of "Colonial Days and Ways" and other valuable works, is a living descendant of the Sharon pastor.

Daniel Parker, first pastor at Ellsworth, a parish in Sharon, was the father of the Hon. Amasa J. Parker, LL.D. Born in Ellsworth, Connecticut, in 1807, he was graduated at Union College in 1825. He was elected to the Legislature of New York in 1833, and two years later was made a regent of the State University. In 1837 he was elected to Congress. In 1844 he became a circuit judge and vice-chancellor of the Court of Equity, and soon afterward judge of the Supreme Court.

The Rev. John W. Beecher, pastor in Ellsworth from 1841 to 1847, had three sons in the Presbyterian ministry, one of whom is the Rev. Willis Judson Beecher, D.D., LL.D., of Auburn Theological Seminary, recognized as one of the leading Biblical exegetes of our time.

The Rev. D. D. T. McLaughlin, pastor in Sharon from 1859 to 1865, and afterward in Litchfield and Morris, had a son of great promise, Edward T. McLaughlin, who was Assistant Professor of English in Yale College, and the author of "Literary Criticism for Students," published by Henry Holt & Co., 1893. His early death was felt as a great loss to literature and scholarship.

The Rev. James Russell Bourne, pastor in Sharon from 1880 to 1890, had two sons, both of whom were prominent in educational work, Edward G. Bourne, late Professor of History at Yale University, and Henry E. Bourne, Professor in Western Reserve University, Cleveland, Ohio. The recent death of Professor E. G. Bourne, while this manuscript was in preparation, was felt as a blow to the cause of historical research.

The Rev. Jeremiah Day, pastor of the church in New Preston from 1769 to 1806, had four sons. The Rev. Jeremiah Day, D.D., LL.D., was Professor of Mathematics and Natural Philosophy at Yale and afterward President of Yale College from 1817 to 1846. The Hon. Thomas Day, LL.D., of Hartford, was Secretary of the State of Connecticut for nearly thirty years. The Rev. Mills Day was tutor at Yale, and Colonel Noble Day was a merchant in New Preston, and father of the Rev. Henry Noble Day, D.D., LL.D., pastor at Waterbury, Connecticut, from 1836 to 1840, Professor of Sacred Rhetoric for eighteen years in Western Reserve College, and afterward President of the Ohio Female College. He was the author of several books of an educational or philosophical character.

Professor Bernadotte Perrin, Ph.D., LL.D., of Yale University, is a son of the Rev. Lavalette Perrin, D.D.,

THE CLERGY OF LITCHFIELD COUNTY

pastor in Goshen from 1843 to 1857, and afterward in Torrington.

The Rev. Cornelius L. Kitchel, pastor for several years in Salisbury, and since professor at Yale University, is a son of the Rev. Harvey Kitchel, D.D., pastor in Thomaston from 1839 to 1848, and afterward President of Middlebury College.

The Rev. Ammi Ruhamah Robbins gave three of his thirteen children to the ministry. One of them was the Rev. Thomas Robbins, D.D., well known as pioneer home missionary, author, book-collector, and librarian at Hartford.

Daniel Farrand, pastor in Canaan for fifty-one years, had a son and a son-in-law who were judges of the Supreme Court in Vermont.

The Rev. Nathaniel Lee, first pastor in Salisbury, the Rev. Samuel J. Mills of Torringford, and the Rev. Publius Vergilius Bogue of Winchester have had three generations of descendants in the ministry. That the ministry is constantly recruited from the families of ministers proves that those best acquainted with the trials and difficulties of a pastor's life believe it to be worth the cost.

When ministers' children are spoken of, the family of Dr. Lyman Beecher, pastor in Litchfield from 1810 to 1826, naturally takes the place of acknowledged pre-eminence. The story is too well known to call for a long

MINISTERS' CHILDREN

recital here. Six sons were all ministers, and all men of marked ability. Edward Beecher, D.D., commanded high respect for his attainments in scholarship, and carried on his preaching and pastoral services to an unusually great age. Thomas K. Beecher, D.D., was for forty-six years pastor at Elmira, New York, and built up a strong church by original methods. He was a pioneer in the institutional church work which has gained such prestige in our day. Henry Ward Beecher easily has the first place among preachers of the nineteenth century. Harriet Beecher Stowe takes first rank among American novelists. Catherine Beecher was a pioneer in the higher education of women, and an author of educational works which had a wide influence. Isabella Beecher Hooker was Connecticut's most prominent woman's suffragist.

If my information in regard to the families of Litchfield County ministers were as extensive as my ignorance, it would be very easy to enlarge this chapter to a book. It would be difficult to find a community in which many of the leading and most influential citizens are not descended from the families of ministers. I have no doubt that if all the facts could be properly collected and presented, so that all might know what the world owes to the children of ministers, the public would be glad to pay the life salaries of country ministers for the sake of this product alone, and that great philanthropists would be eager to provide the means for educating the children of all country pastors. It is possible, however, that in this way clerical life would be made so much easier and more luxurious that the family fiber would be weakened, and deteriorate in quality. On the whole, it may be that greater publicity in this matter would not be desirable.

APPENDIX

AUTHORITIES CONSULTED

Contributions to the Ecclesiastical History of Connecticut.
Minutes of the General Association and General Conference of Connecticut.
Records of the Litchfield County Associations, Consociations, and Monthly Conventions.
Centennial Papers, published by the General Conference of Connecticut, 1876.
Congregational Year Books.
Catalogues of Yale University.
Diary of Thomas Robbins, D.D. (Boston, 1886).
History of Litchfield County (J. W. Lewis & Co., Philadelphia, 1881).
Annals of Winchester (John Boyd, 1876).
History of Torrington (Samuel Orcutt, 1878).
History of Goshen (A. G. Hibbard, 1897).
Cothren's History of Ancient Woodbury.
History of Sharon (C. S. Sedgwick).
History of Cornwall (T. S. Gold).

THE CLERGY OF LITCHFIELD COUNTY

History of Ellsworth (G. F. Goodenough, 1900).
History of Connecticut (Trumbull).
History of Norfolk (Crissey).
Connecticut Evangelical Magazine.
Christian Spectator.
The New Englander.
Bellamy's Works (3 vols., edited by the Rev. Noah Benedict).
Sermons by Backus, by Griffin, by Lathrop.
Autobiographies of Lyman Beecher and Charles G. Finney.
Concise Cyclopedia of Religious Knowledge (Elias B. Sanford, D.D., LL.D.).
Poganuc People and Old Town Folks (Harriet Beecher Stowe).
Sketches of Church Life in Colonial Connecticut (Lucy C. Jarvis).
Colonial Days and Ways (Helen Evertson Smith, Century Co., 1900).
Sermons, and Trial of Virtue (Chauncey Lee, D.D.).
Volumes of Selected Sermons (1798 and 1812).
Sermons in National Preacher.
Works of Horace Bushnell, and Biography.
Proceedings at the Litchfield County Centennial.
Addresses at the Centennial, and the One Hundred and Fiftieth Anniversary of the Consociations of Litchfield County.
Sprague's Annals of the American Pulpit.
Samuel J. Mills, Missionary Pathfinder (Thomas C. Richards, 1906).
Reports of Anniversaries and Other Items from the Litchfield Enquirer, Winsted Herald, New Milford Gazette, Newtown Bee, Connecticut Western News, Hartford Courant, Torrington Register.

APPENDIX

Sermons or Addresses on Special Occasions by Cotton Mather Smith, Ammi R. Robbins, Ebenezer Porter, D.D., Stanley Griswold, Ralph Emerson, D.D., Joseph Eldridge, D.D., Frederick Marsh, Adam Reid, D.D., Lavalette Perrin, D.D., James H. Dill, William E. Bassett, Hiram Eddy, D.D., C. L. Kitchel, William H. Moore, John C. Goddard, Edward C. Starr, and others.

LISTS OF CONGREGATIONAL MINISTERS

THE plan of the following lists is to arrange under each town the pastors of each church, in chronological order, with dates as far as known, followed by names of ministers who by birth or training may be considered as belonging to the town. It is not probable that accuracy or completeness has been attained.

BARKHAMSTED

Pastors	Called	Dismissed	Died
Ozias Eells	1787		1813
Elihu Mason	1814	1817	
Saul Clark	1819	1829	
William R. Gould	1832	1838	
Reuben S. Hazen	1843	1849	
William Goodwin	1849	1850	
Aaron Gates	1850		1850
Hugh Gibson	1850	1852	
A. B. Collins	1852	1853	
Platt T. Holley	1853	1855	
	1874	1876	

THE CLERGY OF LITCHFIELD COUNTY

BARKHAMSTED—Continued

Pastors	Called	Dismissed	Died
F. Norwood	1855	1857	
T. E. Roberts	1858	1859	
John Elliott	1861	1863	
H. N. Galt	1863	1866	
John R. Freeman	1868	1871	
R. Henry Gidman	1871	1873	
Aaron B. Peffers	1877	1880	
Joseph B. Clarke	1881	1888	
Ursinus Olevianus Mohr	1890	1892	
Augustus Alvord	1892	1903	
W. L. Linaberry	1903	1905	
Henry F. Burdon	1905	1907	
Jacob L. Hartsell	1909		

BARKHAMSTED (RIVERTON)

	Called	Dismissed	Died
Luther H. Barber	1843	1861	1908
Winthrop H. Phelps	1861	1863	
Platt T. Holley	1863	1868	
	1872	1874	
Joseph W. Hartshorne	1869	1871	
Frank C. Potter			
M. C. Wood			
W. W. Leete, D.D.			
David J. Ogden			
Rolla S. Bugbee	1879	1880	
Francis H. Viets	1882	1887	
Frank J. Nute	1887	1888	

APPENDIX

BARKHAMSTED (RIVERTON)—Continued

Pastors	Called	Dismissed	Died
Frank P. Waters	1888	1891	
Clay Dent Chunn	1891	1892	
George E. Lincoln	1892	1894	
W. W. Davidson	1895	1896	
George S. Richards	1896		

BETHLEHEM

	Called	Dismissed	Died
Joseph Bellamy, D.D.	1738		1789
Azel Backus, D.D.	1791	1813	1816
John Langdon	1816	1825	1830
Benjamin F. Stanton	1825	1829	1843
Paul Couch	1829	1834	
Fosdick Harrison	1835	1850	1858
Aretas G. Loomis	1850	1860	
Ephraim M. Wright	1861	1865	
George Wallace Banks	1866	1874	
S. Fielder Palmer	1875	1878	
William E. Bassett	1879	1885	
Cornelius W. Morrow	1885	1886	
John P. Trowbridge	1888	1892	
Reginald B. Bury	1893	1894	
Edward P. Ayer	1894	1898	
Adam R. Lutz	1899	1902	
Roy M. Houghton	1903	1905	
Charles M. Good	1906		

THE CLERGY OF LITCHFIELD COUNTY

MINISTERS RAISED UP

Robert Crane
Charles Prentice
Homer Prentice
Dwight C. Stone
David Brown
Benjamin C. Meigs

Frederick Munson
Winfred C. Rhodes
Moses Raymond
Julius Steele
Newell M. Calhoun

BRIDGEWATER

Pastors	Called	Dismissed	Died
Reuben Taylor	1810	1815	
Fosdick Harrison	1824	1829	
	1854	1858	
Maltby Gelston	1831	1832	
Samuel Hume	1832	1833	
Albert B. Camp	1834	1843	
James Kilbourne	1843	1850	
Dillon Williams	1850	1853	
Lemuel S. Potwin	1860	1863	
Henry G. Hunt	1863	1866	
William T. Dean	1866	1871	
John Birge Doolittle	1872	1878	
S. Fielder Palmer	1879	1880	
Eugene F. Atwood	1881	1883	
John E. Elliott	1884	1886	
Louis F. Burgess	1888	1891	
Frank B. Doane	1893	1894	
John Owen Jones	1894	1896	

APPENDIX

BRIDGEWATER—Continued

Pastors	Called	Dismissed	Died
William W. Wallace	1896	1897	
Warren Morse	1897	1900	
Fred W. Raymond	1901	1902	
Dempster D. Gorton	1902	1906	
Harry Davenport	1907		

MINISTERS RAISED UP

Joseph Treat
Isaac C. Beach
Albert E. Dunning, D.D.
William A. Hawley

Julius O. Beardsley
Levi Smith
Philo R. Hurd

CANAAN

Pastors	Called	Dismissed	Died
Elisha Webster	1740	1752	
Daniel Farrand	1752		1803
Charles Prentice	1804		1838
Edward B. Emerson	1841	1843	
Harley Goodwin	1845	1854	1855
Isaac DeVoe	1855	1856	
Henry Snyder	1858	1860	
E. Frank Howe	1862	1865	
Edwin N. Andrews	1865	1867	
William H. Teel	1867	1869	
[1] Joseph E. Swallow	1870	1873	
Edwin Hull	1873	1874	

[1] Simultaneous.

THE CLERGY OF LITCHFIELD COUNTY

CANAAN—Continued

Pastors	Called	Dismissed	Died
[1] Nathaniel G. Bonney	1874	1876	
[1] Joseph A. Tomlinson	1876	1877	
[1] Daniel M. Moore	1878	1888	
[1] Charles Wesley Hanna	1889	1901	
[1] John Lewis Evans	1901	1903	
[1] Arthur F. Hertell	1904	1905	
[1] J. Fraser Evans	1907	1908	
[1] Park A. Bradford	1908		

MINISTERS RAISED UP

Charles F. Prentice
Lyman Prindle
Cyrus Prindle

Robert Campbell
Cyrus G. Prindle

CANAAN (FALLS VILLAGE)

Pastors	Called	Dismissed	Died
Henry A. Russell	1858	1859	
John Edgar	1859	1866	
Henry B. Mead	1869	1870	
[1] Joseph E. Swallow	1870	1873	
[1] Nathaniel G. Bonney	1873	1876	
[1] Joseph A. Tomlinson	1876	1877	
F. J. Grimes	1877	1878	
[1] Daniel M. Moore	1878	1888	
[1] Charles W. Hanna	1889	1901	

[1] Simultaneous.

APPENDIX

CANAAN (FALLS VILLAGE)—CONTINUED

Pastors	Called	Dismissed	Died
[1] J. Lewis Evans	1901	1903	
[1] Arthur F Hertell	1904	1906	
[1] J. Fraser Evans	1907	1908	
[1] Park A. Bradford	1908		

COLEBROOK

	Called	Dismissed	Died
Jonathan Edwards, D.D.	1795	1799	1801
Chauncey Lee, D.D.	1800	1828	1842
Azariah Clark	1830		1832
Edward R. Tyler	1833	1836	1848
Alfred E. Ives	1838	1848	
James R. Mershon	1850	1852	
Archibald Geikie	1854	1863	
Joel Grant	1867	1868	
Henry A. Russell	1868	1877	
Joseph B. Clarke	1878	1884	
J. W. Hartshorne	1884	1887	
Daniel M. Moore	1888	1894	
Benjamin A. Dean	1895	1901	
William Hedges	1901		

MINISTERS RAISED UP

Chauncey G. Lee
John P. Cowles
Gilbert Stocking
Charles Rockwell

Joel Grant
Joel S. Ives
Henry Cowles, D.D.
William H. Gilbert

[1] Simultaneous.

THE CLERGY OF LITCHFIELD COUNTY

CORNWALL (FIRST)

Pastors	Called	Dismissed	Died
Solomon Palmer	1741	1754	
Hezekiah Gold, Jr.	1755		1790
Hercules Weston	1792	1803	1831
Timothy Stone	1803	1827	1852
William Andrews	1827		1838
Nathaniel M. Urmston	1838	1840	
Hiram Day	1844	1848	
Ralph Smith	1851	1854	
Ira Pettibone	1854	1857	
Stephen Fenn	1859	1867	
Elias B. Sanford, D.D., LL.D.	1869	1871	
Newell A. Prince	1872	1874	
Samuel G. White, D.D.	1875	1884	
Henry B. Mead	1885	1886	
Oscar J. McIntire	1886	1887	
Edward Comfort Starr	1888		

CORNWALL (SECOND)

Pastors	Called	Dismissed
Samuel Bird		
John Cornwall		
Israel Holley	1795	1801
Josiah Hawes	1805	1813
Grove L. Brownell	1817	1818
Walter Smith	1819	1838
S. J. Nacy	1838	1839
Joshua L. Maynard	1841	1852
William B. Clarke	1855	1859

APPENDIX

CORNWALL (SECOND)—CONTINUED

Pastors	Called	Dismissed	Died
Charles Wetherby	1859	1866	
Jesse Brush	1867	1873	
Charles N. Fitch	1873	1882	1905
Wayland Spalding	1882	1883	
William H. McDougal	1884	1887	
John Pierpont	1888	1897	
Chester A. Ferris	1897	1901	
Carl Stackman	1902	1905	

MINISTERS RAISED UP

First Church

William Bonney
William Watson Andrews
E. Warren Andrews
William Jackson, D.D.
Thomas R. Gold

E. B. Andrews
Cornelius B. Everitt
Lucius C. Rouse
Samuel J. Andrews, D.D.
T. D. P. Stone

Second Church

John C. Hart
Henry G. Pendleton
Almon B. Pratt

Samuel Scoville
Henry Wadsworth
Dwight M. Pratt, D.D.

GOSHEN

Pastors	Called	Dismissed	Died
Stephen Heaton	1740	1753	1788
Abel Newell	1755	1781	1813

THE CLERGY OF LITCHFIELD COUNTY

GOSHEN—Continued

Pastors	Called	Dismissed	Died
Josiah Sherman	1783	1789	
Asahel Hooker	1791	1810	1813
Joseph Harvey	1810	1825	
Francis H. Case	1826	1828	
Grant Powers	1829		1841
Lavalette Perrin, D.D.	1845	1857	
Joel T. Bingham	1859	1860	
William T. Doubleday	1864	1871	
Timothy A. Hazen	1872	1882	
Daniel B. Lord	1883	1888	
Augustine G. Hibbard	1890	1896	
Harry E. Small	1897		

GOSHEN (NORTH GOSHEN)

Allen McLean	1807	
George Carrington	1829	1833
Guy C. Sampson	1836	1837
C. G. Tracy	1837	1839
Chester Colton	1839	1846
Fred Marsh	1846	1847

MINISTERS RAISED UP

Noah Wadhams
Edward W. Hooker, D.D.
Darius O. Griswold
William Thompson, D.D.
James Beach
Abraham Baldwin, D.D.

APPENDIX

MINISTERS RAISED UP—CONTINUED

Reuben Parmalee
Orlo Bartholomew
Luther Hart
Augustus Thompson, D.D.
A. T. Norton
Theron Baldwin, D.D.

Elisha Parmalee
Ephraim Lyman
Mark Ives
Luther H. Beecher, D.D.
John F. Norton

HARWINTON

Pastors	Called	Dismissed	Died
Timothy Woodbridge	1735	1737	1776
Andrew Bartholomew	1738	1774	1817
David Perry	1774	1783	
Joshua Williams	1790	1822	1835
George E. Pierce, D.D.	1822	1834	
R. M. Chipman	1835	1839	
Charles Bentley	1839	1850	
Warren G. Jester	1850	1853	
Jacob G. Miller	1854	1857	
John A McKinstry	1857	1863	
Robert T. Searle	1864	1865	
Charles H. Bissell	1865	1866	
George Curtis, D.D.	1866	1876	
William N. Meserve	1878	1880	
Thomas Douglass	1880	1883	
Alexander Hall	1883	1885	
Eugene F. Atwood	1886	1887	
Frederick E. Snow	1888	1890	
Willis M. Cleaveland	1891	1892	

THE CLERGY OF LITCHFIELD COUNTY

HARWINTON—Continued

Pastors	Called	Dismissed	Died
William Hedges	1894	1899	
Charles B. Strong	1900	1905	
J. G. W. Herold	1905	1907	
Benjamin P. Capshaw	1907		

MINISTERS RAISED UP

Norris Buell, D.D.
Jacob Catlin, D.D.
David Perry
Abner Wilcox
David Butler, D.D.
Russell Catlin

Rodney Rossiter
Richard Chester
Simeon Catlin
Clement Merriam
H. C. Abernethy
Richard C. Bristol

KENT

Pastors	Called	Dismissed	Died
Cyrus Marsh	1741	1755	
Joel Bordwell	1758		1811
Asa Blair	1813		1823
Laurens P. Hickok, D.D.	1823	1829	
William W. Andrews	1834	1849	
William W. Page	1853	1854	
Elisha Whittlesey	1856	1858	
Evarts Scudder	1859	1866	
Edward P. Payson	1867	1871	
Arthur Crosby	1872	1873	

APPENDIX

KENT—Continued

Pastors	Called	Dismissed	Died
Thomas D. Barclay	1873	1878	
Juba Howe Vorce	1879	1883	
Elbert S. Porter	1883	1888	
Benjamin Mead Wright	1889	1896	
Herbert K. Job	1898	1908	
George Curtis, D.D.			
Clarence H. Perry	1909		

MINISTERS RAISED UP

Samuel J. Mills Birdsey G. Northrup
Edmund Mills Walter Smith
Seth Swift

LITCHFIELD

Pastors	Called	Dismissed	Died
Timothy Collins	1723	1752	1776
Judah Champion	1753		1810
Dan Huntington	1798	1809	
Lyman Beecher, D.D.	1810	1826	
Daniel L. Carroll, D.D.	1827	1829	
Laurens P. Hickok, D.D.	1829	1836	
Jonathan Brace, D.D.	1838	1844	
Benjamin L. Swan	1846	1856	
Leonard W. Bacon, D.D.	1856	1859	
George Richards	1861	1865	
William B. Clarke	1866	1869	
Henry M. Elliott	1870	1874	

THE CLERGY OF LITCHFIELD COUNTY

LITCHFIELD—Continued

Pastors	Called	Dismissed	Died
Allen B. McLean	1875	1881	
Charles Symington	1883	1893	
John Hutchins	1895		

LITCHFIELD (NORTHFIELD)

	Called	Died
Joseph Eleazer Camp	1795	1837
J. S. Dickinson	1844	1851
Lewis Jessup	1851	1854
Noah Coe	1854	1856
Stephen Rogers	1856	1859
James Richards, D.D.	1859	1860
Erastus Colton	1861	1864
Hiram N. Gates	1866	1871
Elias B. Sanford, D.D., LL.D.	1871	1873
William Howard	1875	1876
H. Augustus Ottmann	1877	1881
Edward Comfort Starr	1881	1888
Joseph Kyte	1888	1893
Fred Louis Grant	1895	1905
Giles Frederic Goodenough	1907	

LITCHFIELD (MILTON)

	Called	Died
Benjamin Judd	1802	1804
Abraham Fowler	1807	1813
Asahel Nettleton, D.D.	1813	
Levi Smith	1825	

APPENDIX

LITCHFIELD (MILTON)—Continued

Pastors	Called	Dismissed	Died
Ralph Smith	1841	1844	
John F. Norton	1844	1849	
Herman L. Vaill	1849	1851	
Francis Williams	1851	1853	
James Noyes	1853	1854	
George J. Harrison	1854	1893	
Aurelian Post	1894	1895	
Wesley E. Page	1896	1903	
Joseph D. Prigmore	1904	1906	
Pearl E. Mathias	1906	1907	
Thomas Abner Williams	1908		

MINISTERS RAISED UP

Charles Wadsworth, D.D.
Ethan Osborn
George Beecher
Thomas K. Beecher, D.D.
Oscar Bissell
Almon B. Pratt
Benjamin Osborn
Charles L. Bunce
Holland Weeks
J. Newton Woodruff
Wallace Warner
Lewis Munger
William J. Peck
David L. Parmalee
Edward P. Abbe

Charles Beecher
James Beecher
Ambrose Collins
James Kilbourne
Fred R. Abbe
John Churchill
Jeremiah Woodruff
George C. Woodruff
William H. Guernsey
Isaac Warner
—— McNeil
Edward Beecher, D.D.
Henry Ward Beecher, D.D.
Edward Nolan
Stephen Mason

THE CLERGY OF LITCHFIELD COUNTY

MINISTERS RAISED UP—CONTINUED

Herman L. Vaill
Horace Bushnell, D.D.
Hezekiah B. Pierpont
Lewis H. Woodruff

Noah Bishop
Lewis Smith
Albert B. Camp

MORRIS

Pastors	Called	Dismissed	Died
George Beckwith	1772	1781	
Amos Chase	1787	1814	
William R. Weeks, D.D.	1815	1816	
Amos Pettingill	1816	1822	
Henry Robinson	1823	1829	
Vernon D. Taylor	1831	1833	
James F. Warner	1833	1834	
Ralph S. Crampton	1834	1836	
Stephen Hubbell	1836	1837	
B. Y. Messenger	1837	1838	
Richard Woodruff	1838	1841	
David L. Parmalee	1841	1859	
H. H. McFarland	1859	1861	
Cyrus W. Pickett	1864	1866	
D. D. T. McLaughlin	1867	1871	
Richard Gidman	1872	1875	
Edwin Leonard	1875	1892	
Charles C. Redgrave	1895	1898	
F. A. Holden	1898	1902	
Francis W. Fletcher	1903		

APPENDIX

MINISTERS RAISED UP

Samuel Whittlesey John W. Peck, D.D.
Simeon Woodruff John Pierpont
Samuel G. Orton

NEPAUG

Pastors	Called	Dismissed	Died
Augustus Smith	1849	1851	
James Clay Houghton	1851	1854	
Edwin Hall	1854	1869	
Brown Emerson	1869	1870	
J. N. Woodruff	1870	1871	
Stephen A. Loper	1872	1874	
Merrick Knight	1875	1880	
Richard Scoles	1880	1883	
E. C. Haynes	1884	1885	
Vergil W. Blackman	1885	1887	
William Miller	1887	1890	
J. Lewis Evans	1891	1892	
Charles H. Stevens	1892	1895	
William H. Gay	1895	1896	
G. F. Goodenough	1896	1898	
Malan H. Wright	1898	1903	
Grace Edwards	1903		

MINISTERS RAISED UP

Peter A. Brinsmade Frederick Marsh
Horace Tracy Pitkin John B. Lyman
Solomon J. Douglas

THE CLERGY OF LITCHFIELD COUNTY

NEW HARTFORD

Pastors	Called	Dismissed	Died
Jonathan Marsh	1739	1794	
Edward Dorr Griffin, D.D.	1795	1801	1837
Amasa Jerome	1802	1813	
Cyrus Yale	1814		1854

NEW HARTFORD (NORTH CHURCH)

Burr Baldwin	1829	1833
Willis Lord	1834	1838
John Woodbridge, D.D.	1839	1842
Hiram Day	1842	1844
Alexander Leadbetter	1844	1849
Joseph A. Saxton	1850	1852
Franklin A. Spencer	1853	1863
James B. Cleaveland	1863	1867
Alpheus Winter	1868	1870
Sanford S. Martyn	1870	1874
Fred H. Adams	1875	1887
John P. Hawley	1888	1898
Frank S. Brewer	1898	1906
Edward O. Grisbrook	1907	

NEW MILFORD

Daniel Boardman	1716		1744
Nathanael Taylor	1748		1800
Stanley Griswold	1790	1802	

APPENDIX

NEW MILFORD—Continued

Pastors	Called	Dismissed	Died
Andrew Eliot	1808		1829
Heman Rood	1830	1835	
Noah Porter, D.D., LL.D.	1836	1842	
John Greenwood	1844	1849	
David Murdock, D.D.	1850	1869	
James Bonar	1870	1883	
George S. Thrall	1884	1885	
Timothy J. Lee	1885	1888	
Frank A. Johnson	1889	1907	
George H. Johnson	1908		

MINISTERS RAISED UP

John Treat Baldwin
John Stephens
Benjamin Wildman
Nathanael W. Taylor, D.D.
Daniel Marsh
Gideon Bostwick
Elizur Beecher
Asahel Bronson
Whitman Welch
David Bronson

Orlo D. Hine
Charles Boardman
George Ladd
David Sanford
David Baldwin
Joseph Treat
Merritt S. Platt
David Bostwick
George Sterling

NORFOLK

Pastors	Called	Dismissed	Died
Ammi Ruhamah Robbins	1761		1813
Ralph Emerson, D.D.	1815	1829	

THE CLERGY OF LITCHFIELD COUNTY

NORFOLK—Continued

Pastors	Called	Dismissed	Died
Joseph Eldridge, D.D.	1832	1874	1875
John Wickliffe Beach	1874	1876	
John F. Gleason	1876	1885	
John DePeu	1885	1897	
William F. Stearns	1897		

MINISTERS RAISED UP

Thomas Robbins, D.D.
Nathan Turner
Joseph L. Mills
Asahel Gaylord
Frederick T. Persons
James W. Robbins
Eleazur Holt

Sheridan Guiteau
Reuben Gaylord
Francis LeBaron Robbins
Isaac Knapp
Ira Pettibone
Joseph F. Gaylord

NORTH CANAAN (EAST CANAAN)

Pastors	Called	Dismissed	Died
Asahel Hart	1770		1775
Amos Thompson	1782	1788	
Joshua Knapp	1791	1795	
Solomon Morgan	1798		1804
Pitkin Cowles	1805		1833
Henry H. Woodbridge	1833	1842	
Daniel D. Francis	1844	1850	
Elisha Whittlesey	1851	1853	
Hiram Eddy, D.D.	1856	1860	
Henry M. Grant	1863	1866	

APPENDIX

NORTH CANAAN (EAST CANAAN)—CONTINUED

Pastors	Called	Dismissed	Died
Isaac P. Powell	1868	1874	
Lewis G. Reid	1874	1879	
William Thompson	1882	1884	
Eugene F. Atwood	1884	1886	
Horace G. Hoadley	1886	1891	
Henry Utterwick	1891	1900	
Charles Wesley Hanna	1901		

NORTH CANAAN (PILGRIM)

Dwight C. Stone	1888
Charles D. Milliken	1892
Sidney A. Burnaby	1897
Edwin C. Gillette	1902

MINISTERS RAISED UP

Grove L. Brownell
Zalmon Tobey
Linus Fellowes

Timothy Benedict
Aaron Peale
Calvin Peale

PLYMOUTH

Pastors	Called	Dismissed	Died
Samuel Todd	1740	1764	1789
Andrew Storrs	1765		1785
Joseph Badger	1786	1787	

THE CLERGY OF LITCHFIELD COUNTY

PLYMOUTH—Continued

Pastors	Called	Dismissed	Died
Simon Waterman	1787	1809	1813
Luther Hart	1810		1834
Ephraim Lyman	1835	1851	
Israel P. Warren, D.D.	1851	1856	
Erskine J. Hawes	1858		1860
Robert C. Learned	1861	1865	
Henry E. Cooley	1866	1869	
Elias B. Hillard	1869	1889	
John Sheridan Zelie, D.D.	1890	1894	
Charles H. Smith	1895	1903	
Edwin J. Lewis	1904	1907	
Theodore B. Lathrop	1908		

PLYMOUTH (TERRYVILLE)

Nathaniel Richardson	1838	1840
Merrill Richardson	1841	1846
	1849	1858
Judson A. Root	1846	1847
John Monteith	1858	1860
A. Hastings Ross		
Edwin R. Dimock	1861	1862
Franklin A. Spencer	1863	1865
E. M. Wright	1866	1870
Henry B. Mead	1871	1874
Leverett S. Griggs	1874	1887
William F. Arms	1888	1893
William A. Gay	1893	1902
Spencer E. Evans	1902	

APPENDIX

MINISTERS RAISED UP

Edwin Johnson Moseley H. Williams
Linus Blakeslee Horace R. Williams

ROXBURY

Pastors	Called	Dismissed	Died
Thomas Canfield	1774		1795
Zephaniah Swift	1795	1812	1848
Fosdic Harrison	1813	1835	1858
Austin Isham	1839	1863	
Oliver S. Dean, D.D.	1864	1867	
Arthur Goodenough	1869	1870	
David E. Jones	1871	1887	
H. H. Morse	1887	1888	
George H. Burgess	1888	1889	
Mosheim R. Fishburn	1890	1891	
J. Jones Vaughan	1893	1895	
George A. Bushee	1896	1900	
Alfred E. Thistleton	1901	1903	
Clay Dent Chunn	1905	1908	

MINISTERS RAISED UP

David B. Davidson

SALISBURY

Pastors	Called	Dismissed	Died
Jonathan Lee	1743		1788
William F. Miller	1790		

THE CLERGY OF LITCHFIELD COUNTY

SALISBURY—Continued

Pastors	Called	Dismissed	Died
John Eliot	1791		
James Glossbrook	1792	1793	
Ebenezer Porter, D.D.	1795		
Timothy M. Cauley, D.D.	1795		
Joseph W. Crossman	1796		1812
John B. Whittlesey	1812	1813	
William R. Weeks, D.D.	1814	1815	1848
Chauncey A. Goodrich, D.D.	1815		
Federal Burt	1816		
Lavius Hyde	1817	1822	
William C. Fowler	1823		
L. E. Lathrop, D.D.	1825	1836	1857
Adam Reid, D.D.	1836	1877	
Cornelius L. Kitchel	1877	1883	
John Calvin Goddard	1884		

MINISTERS RAISED UP

James Hutchinson
Chauncey Lee, D.D.
Henry P. Strong
Edmund Janes
Joseph Pettee
Eliphalet Whittlesey
Samuel Camp
Horace Holley, D.D.

William L. Strong
Josiah Turner
Henry Pratt
Isaac Bird
George A. Calhoun, D.D.
Edward Hollister
Edwin Holmes
Elisha Whittlesey

APPENDIX

SHARON

Pastors	Called	Dismissed	Died
Peter Pratt	1740	1747	1780
John Searl	1749	1754	1787
Cotton Mather Smith	1755		1806
David L. Perry	1804		1835
Mason Grosvenor	1836	1837	
Grove L. Brownell	1840	1848	
Charles Rockwell	1850	1851	
Thomas G. Corner	1851	1853	
Leonard E. Lathrop, D.D.	1854		1857
D. D. T. McLaughlin	1859	1886	
A. B. Bullions, D.D.	1868	1878	
James R. Bourne	1880	1889	
Gerald Stanley Lee	1889	1893	
Edward O. Dyer	1893	1906	
Allyn K. Foster	1906	1907	
Gilbert L. Forte	1907		

SHARON (ELLSWORTH)

Daniel Parker	1802	1812	1832
Orange Lyman	1813	1816	1851
Frederick Gridley	1820	1836	
John W. Beecher	1841	1847	1858
William W. Baldwin	1849	1851	
William J. Alger	1852	1853	
Porter B. Parry	1853	1857	
Robert D. Gardner	1858	1865	

THE CLERGY OF LITCHFIELD COUNTY

SHARON (ELLSWORTH)—Continued

Pastors	Called	Dismissed	Died
Arthur Goodenough	1865	1869	
Oscar Bissell	1869	1870	
Andrew Montgomery	1870	1872	
William Terrett	1872	1873	
John O. Stevenson, D.D.	1874	1879	
E. C. Hull	1880	1885	
John H. Müller	1886	1889	
E. C. Haynes	1889	1890	
Idrys Jones	1891	1893	
Evore Evans	1894	1897	
G. F. Goodenough	1898	1903	
Wesley E. Page	1903		

MINISTERS RAISED UP

Jeremiah Day
William Jewell
Daniel Smith
David C. Perry
George I. Keach
Jacob Chamberlain
Charles Y. Chase
Gad Smith
Gad Smith, 2d
Vinson Gould
John M. S. Perry
David R. Gould
Charles H. Read
Jesse W. Guernsey

Walter Chamberlain
Alvin Somers
Willis J. Beecher, D.D.
Elisha Frink
Edwin Bailey
James B. Cleaveland
Gilbert L. Smith
Hiram White
William Terrett
Seymour Landon
Thomas Beebe
Milo North Miles
W. Alanson Beecher
William Baldwin

APPENDIX

THOMASTON

Pastors	Called	Dismissed	Died
Harvey D. Kitchell, D.D.	1839	1848	
Joseph D. Hull	1849	1851	
James Averill	1852	1862	
J. B. Pearson			
R. P. Searl			
Joseph W. Backus, D.D.	1867	1878	
H. C. Hitchcock	1879	1880	
S. M. Freeland	1881	1887	
Rolla S. Bugbee	1888	1891	
Robert W. Sharpe	1892	1896	
Austin Hazen	1897		

THOMASTON (EAGLE ROCK)

Elias B. Sanford, D.D., LL.D.	1878	1884	
Dighton Moses	1888	1889	
Lydia Hartig	1905		

THOMASTON (SWEDISH)

Andrew O. Petersen	1892	1893	
Henry Soderholm	1893	1895	
Ferdinand Scholander	1896	1905	
Adolph F. Högberg	1905		

THE CLERGY OF LITCHFIELD COUNTY

TORRINGTON

Pastors	Called	Dismissed	Died
Nathaniel Roberts	1741		1776
Noah Merwin	1776	1783	1795
Lemuel Haynes	1787	1789	1834
Alexander Gillette	1792		1826
William R. Gould	1827	1832	
Milton Huxley	1832	1842	
John A. McKinstry	1842	1857	
Charles B. Dye	1859	1860	
Sylvanus P. Marvin	1860	1865	
Jacob A. Strong	1865	1869	
Michael J. Callan	1870	1872	
Samuel Orcutt	1873	1875	
Charles P. Croft	1876	1879	
Frank F. Jorden	1881	1884	
William F. Hutchins	1884	1886	
Ursinus Olevianus Mohr	1887	1889	
Charles D. Crawford	1889	1891	
E. Chalmers Haynes	1891	1892	
Andrew W. Gerrie	1892	1899	
Thomas C. Richards	1899	1906	
Charles M. Bryant	1906		

TORRINGTON (TORRINGFORD)

Stephen Heaton	1761		
Ebenezer Davenport	1764	1767	
Samuel J. Mills	1769		1833

APPENDIX

TORRINGTON (TORRINGFORD)—Continued

Pastors	Called	Dismissed	Died
Epaphras Goodman	1822	1836	
Herman L. Vaill	1837	1839	
Brown Emerson	1841	1844	
John D. Baldwin	1844	1845	
William H. Moore	1846	1854	
Stephen Fenn	1854	1857	
Charles Newman	1858	1862	
Spencer O. Dyer	1863	1864	
Franklin Noble	1864	1866	
Joseph F. Gaylord	1866	1868	
Dana M. Walcott	1869	1871	
Merrick Knight	1872	1874	
George R. Ferguson	1875	1877	
Chester Bridgeman	1878	1879	
Clarence H. Barber	1880	1887	
Henry C. Robinson	1888	1891	
Austin H. Norris	1892		1903
G. F. Goodenough	1903	1907	
John H. Davis	1908		

TORRINGTON (THIRD, CENTER)

	Called	Dismissed
Henry P. Arms, D.D.	1833	1836
Stephen Hubbell	1837	1839
Samuel Day	1840	1845
Samuel T. Seelye, D.D.	1846	1855
Ralph Smith	1856	1857
E. L. Clarke	1857	1859

THE CLERGY OF LITCHFIELD COUNTY

TORRINGTON (THIRD, CENTER)—Continued

Pastors	Called	Dismissed	Died
George B. Newcomb			
Edward W. Bacon	1869	1871	
Lavalette Perrin, D.D.	1872	1887	
Charles E. Andrews	1887	1889	
Henry B. Roberts	1890	1898	
James A. Chamberlin, D.D.	1899	1901	
Alvin F. Sherrill, D.D.	1901	1902	
Arthur W. Ackerman, D.D.	1902		

TORRINGTON (FRENCH)

Joseph Provost 1897

MINISTERS RAISED UP

Timothy Phelps Gillette
Miles Grant
Stanley Griswold
Orange Lyman
Abel Knapp Hinsdale
David Miller
Jonathan Miller

Samuel J. Mills, Jr.
Lucius Quintus Curtis
Jacob Catlin, D.D.
David B. Lyman
Harvey Loomis
E. D. Moore

WARREN

Pastors	Called	Dismissed	Died
Silvanus Osborn	1757		1771
Peter Starr	1772		1829

APPENDIX

WARREN—Continued

Pastors	Called	Dismissed	Died
Hart Talcott	1825		1836
Harley Goodwin	1838	1843	1855
John R. Keep	1844	1852	
M. M. Wakeman	1853	1856	
Francis Lobdell	1859	1863	
William E. Bassett	1863	1875	
Willis F. Colton	1876	1888	
Austin Gardner	1889	1897	
Myron A. Munson	1898	1903	
William E. Brooks, D.D.	1904	1906	
Charles A. Pickett	1907		

MINISTERS RAISED UP

Reuben Taylor
Prince Hawes
Julian M. Sturtevant, D.D.
Myron N. Marvin
Charles Everitt
Alanson Sanders
Charles G. Finney, D.D.
John S. Griffin

Josiah Hawes
Nathaniel Swift
Urban Palmer
John L. Taylor, D.D.
Lucius C. Rouse
Seth Sackett
Tertius Reynolds

WASHINGTON

Pastors	Called	Dismissed	Died
Reuben Judd	1742	1747	
Daniel Brinsmade	1749		1793
Noah Merwin	1785		1795

THE CLERGY OF LITCHFIELD COUNTY

WASHINGTON—Continued

Pastors	Called	Dismissed	Died
Ebenezer Porter, D.D.	1796	1811	
Cyrus W. Gray	1813	1815	
Stephen Mason	1818	1828	
Gordon Hayes	1829	1851	
Ephraim Lyman	1852	1863	
W. H. H. Murray	1864	1865	
Willis S. Colton	1866	1876	
George L. Thrall	1877	1881	
William Crawford	1882	1883	
Herbert B. Turner, D.D.	1884	1893	
Robert E. Carter	1894		

WASHINGTON (NEW PRESTON)

Noah Wadhams	1757	1768	
Jeremiah Day	1770		1806
Samuel Whittlesey	1807	1817	
Charles A. Boardman	1818	1830	
Robert B. Campfield	1831	1834	
Columbus Shumway	1834	1835	
Merritt S. Platt	1836	1837	
Benjamin B. Parsons	1839	1842	
Hollis Read	1845	1851	
Samuel F. Bacon	1851	1853	
Charles S. Smith	1853	1855	
Joseph A. Saxton	1856	1857	
Jacob A. Strong	1857		
Henry Upson	1863	1872	

APPENDIX

WASHINGTON (NEW PRESTON)—CONTINUED

Pastors	Called	Dismissed	Died
Dighton Moses			
Henry Lancashire	1877	1882	
Frank S. Childs, D.D.	1884	1888	
George W. Davis	1890	1891	
Evan Evans	1894	1898	
Nicholas S. Becker	1900	1901	
Aurelian H. Post	1902	1907	
J. Edward Hermann	1907		

WASHINGTON (NEW PRESTON HILL)

Levi S. Beebe	1854	1855
John A. Hemstead	1855	1856
Noah Coe	1856	1857
William H. Whittemore	1859	1860
George W. Coleman	1862	1863
Lewis Williams	1867	1869
John A. Woodhull	1869	1872
Henry Upson	1873	1877
Austin Isham	1878	1888
George W. Davis	1890	1891
Evan Evans	1894	1898
	1907	

MINISTERS RAISED UP

John Clarke
Bennett B. Burgess
Thomas Knapp

William Sidney Smith
Gideon H. Pond
George Tomlinson

THE CLERGY OF LITCHFIELD COUNTY

MINISTERS RAISED UP—CONTINUED

George Bushnell, D.D.
Daniel Parker
Samuel Pond
George A. Calhoun, D.D.
Augustus Smith
Jeremiah Day, D.D., LL.D.
Charles W. Camp
Johnson L. Tomlinson

Elisha Mitchell
Lewis Gunn
Henry Calhoun
Levi Smith
Henry N. Day, D.D.
Benjamin B. Smith
Joseph Whittlesey
Samuel L. Whittlesey

WATERTOWN

Pastors	Called	Dismissed	Died
John Trumbull	1739		1787
Uriel Gridley	1784		1820
Horace Hooker	1822	1824	
Darius O. Griswold	1825	1835	1841
William B. DeForest	1835	1837	
Philo R. Hurd	1840	1849	
Chauncey Goodrich	1849	1856	
George P. Prudden	1856	1861	
Samuel M. Freeland	1862	1864	
Benjamin Pearson	1865	1867	
Stephen Fenn	1868	1872	
G. A. P. Gilman	1872	1876	
Franklin Tuxbury	1877	1879	
Charles P. Croft	1880		
Benjamin D. Conkling	1881	1884	
George N. Pelton	1886	1889	
Robert Pegrum	1889	1900	
William T. Holmes	1901		

APPENDIX

MINISTERS RAISED UP

Aaron Dutton
Israel Beard Woodward
John L. Seymour
Frederick Gridley
Matthew Rice Dutton

Stephen Fenn
Jesse Guernsey
Anson S. Atwood
Henry DeForest

WINCHESTER

Pastors	Called	Dismissed	Died
Joshua Knapp	1772	1789	1816
Publius Vergilius Bogue	1790	1800	1836
Archibald Bassett	1801	1806	
Thomas Robbins, D.D.	1806	1807	
Frederick Marsh	1808	1851	1873
James H. Dill	1846	1852	
John Cunningham	1852	1854	
Ira Pettibone	1857	1865	
William M. Gay	1866	1869	
Arthur Goodenough	1870		

WINCHESTER (WINSTED, FIRST)

	Called	Dismissed	Died
Ezra Woodworth	1792	1799	
Aaron Kinney	1799	1804	
James Beach	1806	1842	1850
T. M. Dwight	1842	1844	
Augustus Pomeroy	1844	1845	
Ira Pettibone	1846	1854	
Henry A. Russell	1854	1858	

THE CLERGY OF LITCHFIELD COUNTY

WINCHESTER (WINSTED, FIRST)—Continued

Pastors	Called	Dismissed	Died
James B. Pierson	1859	1862	
Malcolm McG. Dana	1862	1865	
J. B. R. Walker	1867	1869	
Henry E. Cooley	1869	1870	
Thomas M. Miles	1870	1879	1908
Timothy J. Lee	1879	1884	
Henry N. Kinney	1884	1894	
George F. Prentiss	1894	1898	
George W. Judson	1898		

WINCHESTER (WINSTED, SECOND)

C. H. A. Buckley	1854	1859
Arthur T. Pierson, D.D.	1859	1860
Hiram Eddy, D.D.	1861	1865
Charles Wetherby	1866	1871
M. B. Angier	1871	1873
Leavitt H. Hallock, D.D.	1873	1883
Henry H. Kelsey	1884	1888
Henry P. Peck	1889	1891
J. Spencer Voorhees	1892	1896
Newell M. Calhoun	1897	1907
Everard W. Snow	1908	

MINISTERS RAISED UP

Noble Everitt
Abel McEwen, D.D.
Samuel Rockwell
Willard Burr
Frederick L. Grant
Daniel E. Goodwin

APPENDIX

MINISTERS RAISED UP—CONTINUED

Henry B. Blake
John W. Alvord
Arthur C. Dill
Giles Frederic Goodenough

Eliphaz Platt
Charles Rockwell
Leuman H. Pease
Thomas C. Richards

WOODBURY

Pastors	Called	Dismissed	Died
Zachariah Walker	1668		1700
Anthony Stoddard	1702		1760
Noah Benedict	1760		1813
Worthington Wright	1811	1813	
Henry P. Strong	1814	1816	
Samuel R. Andrews	1817	1846	1858
Lucius Q. Curtis	1846	1854	
Robert G. Williams	1855	1859	
Charles E. Robinson	1861	1864	
Charles Little	1865	1867	
Horace Winslow	1868	1869	
Gurdon Noyes	1869	1879	
Joseph A. Freeman	1881	1905	1906
Stanley F. Blomfield	1905	1908	
Howard A. Seckerson	1909		

WOODBURY (NORTH CHURCH)

Grove L. Brownell	1817	1840
John Churchill	1840	1869
James L. R. Wyckoff	1871	1908
Charles E. Underwood	1909	

THE CLERGY OF LITCHFIELD COUNTY

MINISTERS RAISED UP

Ephraim Judson
Adoniram Judson, D.D.
Thomas Miner
Justus Mitchell
Philo Judson
Samuel Judson

William P. Curtis
Judson A. Root
Euston Judson
Gould C. Judson
William T. Bacon

www.ingramcontent.com/pod-product-compliance
Lightning Source LLC
Chambersburg PA
CBHW062003220426
43662CB00010B/1219